YOU'RE NOT SINGING ANYMORE!

A riotous celebration of football chants and the culture that spawned them

Adrian Thrills

EBURY
PRESS

First published in Great Britain in 1998

13 5 7 9 10 8 6 4 2

Ebury Press
Random House, 20 Vauxhall Bridge Road, London SW1V 2SA

Random House Australia Pty Limited
20 Alfred Street, Milsons Point, Sydney, New South Wales 2061, Australia

Random House New Zealand Limited
18 Poland Road, Glenfield, Auckland 10, New Zealand

Random House South Africa (Pty) Limited
Endulini, 5A Jubilee Road, Parktown 2193, South Africa

Random House UK Limited Reg. No. 954009

A CIP catalogue record for this book is available from the British Library

ISBN 0 09 186328 7

Cover design by Push, London
Book design by Nigel Davies

Original cover photo © Popperfoto
Other photographs copyright © Colorsport (pp. 9, 15, 41, 57, 63, 83, 143, 155); MSI (pp. 27, 71, 125); PA News (pp. 91, 133); Hulton Getty (pp. 107, 117); Steve Hale (p. 99).

The extract from the sleeve of *The Kop Choir* (p. 34) is used courtesy of Cherry Red Records and the extract from *The Glory Game* by Hunter Davies (p. 35) is courtesy of Mainstream Publishing. The extract from the sleeve of *Keep Right On* is courtesy of Cherry Red Records.

'Good Old Arsenal' was written by Hunter/Hill and is published by Weekend Music.
'Blue Is The Colour' was written by D. Boone/R. McQueen and is published by EMI Music.
'The End of The Road' was written by Lauder/Dillon and is published by Francis Day and Hunter/Redwood Music.
'Follow Follow' was written by Billy King and is published by Mavis Music.

Printed and bound in Great Britain by Mackay's of Chatham, plc

Papers used by Ebury Press are natural, recyclable products made from wood grown in sustainable forests.

CONTENTS

PART ONE
THE STORY

THE SOUND
OF THE CROWD

Everyone can probably remember something of their first football match. The most abiding impressions of the occasion are unlikely to have been the final score, which player notched the opening goal or even who the opposing team were. But something of the day's ultimate flavour should have survived. Maybe it was the smell of chip fat from the hot-dog vans, the whiff of liniment at the players' entrance or the visual treat of seeing the vibrant, verdant hue of a football pitch under floodlights for the first time. Maybe it was the sensation of being passed over crush barriers and older heads, down to the bottom reaches of a giant concrete terrace. Or maybe it was the sound of the crowd that made a lasting impression.

There is nothing quite like the sound of a football crowd in full voice. For a lot of supporters, the racket of a huge section of football fans singing was their first exposure to the sound of music on a mass scale. The majority of people, serious music-lovers included, probably went to a football match long before they attended their first rock, pop or classical concert. And a football match – certainly in the Sixties, the Seventies and for much of the Eighties – meant plenty of singing, shouting and chanting in unison.

It is not that long ago that singing and chanting were arguably *the* most essential ingredients of the average football fan's matchday experience. And while the circumstances might be different at many big grounds in the Nineties, the legacies of the golden years of football chanting live on in most football arenas. Away from the executive boxes, family sections and the overpriced seats of the main stands, significant pockets of singers still prevail at our football grounds. Dedicated zealots, these are the fans who, even in the relatively gentrified atmosphere of the Nineties, still hark back to the age of chants.

Back in the golden years of football chanting, the very foundations of the big grounds would be shaken and rocked by the sound of the songs. Belted out in unison, with admirable disregard for social tact or melodic quality, these songs gave ordinary supporters the opportunity to air their most passionate and absurd concerns. There were songs of praise to the nimble wizards of the wing and anthems that vilified the remarkably ugly centre-half wearing the colours of the opposing side. There were chants that concentrated on the blatant shortcomings of the referee, his need to visit the nearest optician or the fact that the linesman's shorts were three sizes too small. There were limericks based on the opposing captain's alleged weakness for buxom blondes plus whole sonnets about a rival team manager's reported penchant for a bottle of vintage malt on the team coach home. There were songs devised and sung about Geoff Hurst's boots, Joe Jordan's teeth, Jim Holton's eyes, Alan Cork's lack of hair and Paul Gascoigne's expanding waistline. There were songs about everything and songs about nothing.

The chanting used to begin long before kick-off. With fewer fans booking tickets in advance, there was a far bigger onus on getting into the ground early to secure a good vantage point. On the terraces, this meant a place behind a metal crush barrier, ideally behind one of the goals or on one of the massive concrete expanses of side terracing such as the old Shelf at White Hart Lane.

The chanting would start, often up to two hours before the start of the game, with the traditional songs of praise. Then, as the first members of the home side began warming up, specific tributes to individual players would start, each with its own distinct melodic refrain. Flank players would be acclaimed with a variation on the 'Willie, Willie Morgan, Willie Morgan on the wing' chant, sung to the tune of the chorus of 'Gin Gan Goolie' by Liverpool pop group The Scaffold. The utility players, versatile men who were once famously described as being rubbish in more than one position, were usually greeted to the tune of 'The

Quartermaster's Store' and the words '*he's here, he's there, he's every fucking where*'.

Plenty of romantic mythology has grown up around the great singing citadels of British football – from the Kop, Stretford End and the Shed to Ibrox and Parkhead – but that is only understandable in the light of the unique atmosphere that existed at big games in the period from the Sixties through to the early Eighties. Not only did the singing start earlier in the afternoon. It also took hold of huge sections of the stadium with remarkable speed and volume due to the fact that so many supporters were huddled close together.

'In those days, you could *feel* the singing,' says Graeme, a Chelsea fan who stood in The Shed in the Seventies. 'Even a deaf person would have been aware of the noise. There was a vibration that came from that amount of people chanting and clapping. Football matches could be a bit scary in those days, but it was a truly sensational time. Some of the songs had verses and choruses and seemed to go on for ages. A lot of the Chelsea chants would be very derogatory about northerners in the most unsubtle way and many of them weren't even particularly funny. But, when they were being sung in unison by thousands, sometimes tens of thousands of fans, they tended to take on a certain power.

'When you supported a side like Chelsea, it was hard not to get caught up in the sheer adrenalin of the experience, even if that entailed running with the pack to an extent. There was something tremendously exciting about being in a crowd and singing like that. When I meet some of the people I used to go to football with in the Seventies, we will talk about those days like a couple of war veterans. The game is so different now that the songs of those days are becoming a fading memory.'

There is a tendency to talk of a matchday crowd as a single group. But football fans, even those supporting the same team, are not a monolith of identical parts. The crowd can be made up of a number of different factions. Sometimes these will merge into a single voice, but often they will also give voice to their separate personalities. Liverpool fans at the Anfield Road end of the stadium were known to chant '*Koppites are gobshites*' at the occupants of the more famous terrace behind the opposite goal. There have even been differences among sections of the same stand, one famous call-and-response chant at Stamford Bridge being a vocal joust between Chelsea fans in '*the middle of The Shed*' and those just a few feet away beside '*the white wall of The Shed*'.

During the Eighties, *'you're not singing anymore'* was one of the more familiar chants heard at football grounds across the country. Married to the tune of the Welsh hymn 'Bread Of Heaven', it was sung to ridicule rival fans who had been shocked or shamed into silence. This would invariably happen immediately after their team had just conceded a goal. But the silence would never last very long. The fans on the receiving end of the taunt could be relied on to pool their resources and answer the original chant with their own ad-libbed verse. The reply was often *'you only sing when you're winning'*, tethered to the traditional Latin folk song 'Guantanamera'. If the team in question were from a largely rural part of the country, then *'you only sing when you're farming'* would often be sung instead. A team such as Grimsby Town, who hail from a trawling port, would be derided with *'you only sing when you're fishing'*. The variations were countless: whenever one group of supporters chanted *'you're not singing anymore'*, it would always elicit some form of vocal rejoinder from their opposite numbers.

That has not always been the case recently. Now, quite often, the fans don't even sing at all. There are even games where – because of ground improvements and fears of crowd trouble – there are no away fans present, thus ridding the match of the musical tension that was the traditional essence of live football. With football embracing modern ways, there are many who now claim the days of the terrace singalong are numbered.

But the songs have not stopped just yet. The scenes at Wembley during the England games in *Euro 96* were both a throwback to a previous era and a possible pointer to a future rich in its potential for fresh songs and chants. When former Arsenal manager George Graham returned to the game in 1996 after an 18-month sabbatical, he was struck once more by the passion of English crowds. 'It doesn't matter where you go in the world,' Graham told me. 'You can travel all around Europe and you won't find crowds with the same commitment as in Britain. And it's peaking again just now. Whether that passion lasts, only time will tell. But right now, there's nothing like the British game for crowd excitement.'

This book is a celebration of football songs and the culture that spawned them. The first section details the history of the phenomenon and then examines the vital links between football songs and pop culture. It also introduces some of the individuals behind the sounds that still boom out at grounds up and down the land. The second section is a compendium of some of the chants that have prevailed during the four decades since singing in unison became a nationwide phenomenon in the early Sixties. It would be impossible to be totally comprehensive in cataloguing such chants and this second section should be viewed as a selective guide. Many chants have been omitted due to their racist or sectarian content. Some, such as the songs about the Munich Air Disaster that have been directed at Manchester United fans, are absent on grounds of common decency. And others, such as the *'boing, boing, boing, boing'* mantra chanted by West Bromwich Albion supporters during their Wembley play-off victory against Port Vale in 1993 are simply so surreal that the printed page cannot do them justice.

It is a testimony to the endless wit and invention of football supporters that, even without the obscenities, there are still plenty of intriguing and exotic songs worthy of consideration. The roots of some are thoroughly bizarre, the origins of others shrouded in mystery. But, from sticks of celery to wheelbarrows, greasy chip butties to garden sheds and meat pies to seaside piers, some exceedingly strange subjects are tackled in song here. You're not singing anymore? That particular result is still far from being a foregone conclusion.

IT'S COMING HOME

HOME

'Three Lions' — the making of an anthem

Just three weeks before football came home, anyone wandering in the region of Wembley Stadium would have been hard pushed to conclude that England was on the verge of hosting its most prestigious football tournament since the 1966 World Cup. A few bright pennants, featuring Warholian images of a handful of England's past football idols, fluttered from the lamp posts that lined Olympic Way. But, as the faces of Stanley Matthews, Bobby Moore and Gary Lineker looked out across the grey, concrete domain of the Twin Towers and into the London drizzle, the spectre of a colourful sporting and cultural fiesta seemed a long way off.

It was a Saturday afternoon towards the end of May. But, despite the fact that the England team were about to take on Hungary in their final home warm-up match before the more competitive engagements of *Euro 96*, the mood in and around the old stadium gave little indication of what the following weeks might have in store. The fixture was one that was rich in history and tradition. The 3-6 defeat inflicted on England by the Hungarians at Wembley in November 1953 was a landmark match that was stitched into the fabric of English football. It was the encounter that erased the myth of English invincibility at home to European opposition and had such an impact back in Hungary that one of Budapest's most popular drinking haunts was later renamed the 6-3 Bar.

Beneath an overcast sky, however, the atmosphere for the spring 1996 rematch was little short of woeful. The attendance was sparse, so much so that the colour-coded seating at one end of the stadium eerily spelt out the word 'Embley' as the two teams kicked off. And, once the game was underway, the crowd, almost exclusively English fans, still did little to make their passions particularly audible.

The songs which had, in the past, been most readily associated with England's home games were given their dutiful airings. But, even as a side coached by Terry Venables strolled to a routine 3-0 victory over the Hungarians, the renditions of 'Rule Britannia' and 'Land of Hope and Glory' were hardly sung with a communal fervour that was likely to strike fear into the hearts of any prospective *Euro 96* opponents. Much the same was true of the familiar, feeble-minded mantra of '*Ing-Ger-Land, Ing-Ger-Land, Ing-Ger-Land*' that accompanied the victory. From some sections, the songs of xenophobia were also forthcoming. No team from continental Europe ever plays at Wembley without being serenaded with at least one chorus of '*if it wasn't for the English, you'd be Krauts*', and the visit of the Hungarians was no exception. There were also a few versions of 'Swing Low Sweet Chariot'. The latter hymn always sounds out of place at a football ground, having been stolen from the followers of an alien sport, rugby union. Its very presence, however, just three weeks before the start of *Euro 96*, appeared to underline the desperate need among English football fans to have a public anthem to call their own.

Traditionally, followers of English international football haven't been well served by the pop singles recorded by the national side. 'Back Home', the official song for the 1970 World Cup in Mexico, was a relative high point. But, for all its kitsch, cheery grandeur, even that chart-topping single never made the transition from *Top of the Pops* to the terraces. The rest of the 1970s, lamentably, were a complete wasteland, not only in terms of songs, but also in terms of the team's participation in the final stages of the major tournaments. And while on-field fortunes improved in the 1980s, the official singalongs were still all instantly forgettable. Neither the 1982 World Cup song 'This Time We'll Get it Right' nor its 1986 follow-up 'We've Got the Whole World at Our Feet' were hits inside the world's stadia. A similar fate also befell the 1988 European Championship song 'All the Way'. The latter single was notable in retrospect only for its outrageously misplaced optimism, for England were beaten in all three of their group games – against the Republic of Ireland, Holland and the Soviet Union – in West Germany.

The 1990 World Cup in Italy, a watershed in terms of football's popularity in Britain, did finally grant England their first decent team song for two decades. A collaboration between Manchester group New Order, comic Keith Allen and six members of Bobby Robson's *Italia 90* squad – John Barnes, Peter Beardsley, Paul Gascoigne, Steve McMahon, Des Walker and Chris Waddle – it was a superb piece of music. A song that tapped candidly into the summer-of-love mood that prevailed in the aftermath of the acid house boom that swept the nightclubs in the late 1980s, it was right for the time. A huge hit on the dancefloor and in the charts, the song's importance in helping to make football appear stylish once again should never be underplayed.

But, for all its magnificent, celebratory irreverence, 'World in Motion' wasn't actually a football fan's song. It didn't reflect what it was actually like watching England play and thus never took off on the terraces. For that, the England fans – such as those in dire need of an uplifting anthem at the England-Hungary warm-up game – would have to wait until *Euro 96* got properly underway: then they would have 'Three Lions'.

The official England single for *Euro 96*, 'Three Lions' was written and recorded by the Lightning Seeds, an act fronted by former Liverpudlian punk Ian Broudie, and the comedy duo David Baddiel and Frank Skinner of the BBC's *Fantasy Football League* programme. Described by Skinner at the time as an venture in 'optimism with a certain amount of scar tissue', the song attempted to sum up the emotional roller-coaster of supporting England. Rather than be blindly optimistic like previous singles, it acknowledged past failures. But it also balanced the traditional jokes made at England's expense with dreams of future glory and a few dewy-eyed, heartfelt reminders of what past teams had achieved.

The song title had been partly inspired by an interview with the then Newcastle United manager and former England captain Kevin Keegan in *Loaded* magazine. In the feature, Keegan had described the patriotic feeling of playing for England and his own awareness of the three lions on the badge of his shirt. With typically romantic fervour, Keegan was trying to impart to the England squad of 1996 that they were part of an evocative, stirring tradition. For all the embarrassment and humiliation of the World Cup and European Championship defeats at the hands of Czechoslovakia, Poland, Norway, Switzerland, Denmark, Portugal and the Republic Of Ireland that littered the 1970s and 1980s, the story of the England football team was also the tale of Bobby Moore's tackles, Gary Lineker's goals and a toothless Nobby Stiles dancing a jig on the Wembley pitch while holding the Jules Rimet trophy.

'The song is about being an England fan,' Skinner had told rock weekly *New Musical Express* when the single was released. 'But it's also about received opinion. People think it's really clever to say how bad England are. But we nearly got to the 1990 World Cup final in Italy and we reached the quarter-finals in Mexico in 1986 before going out to a foul. I do feel that the England team have got better. So the song admits that we've fucked it up a lot of times in the past, but we mightn't fuck it up this time. If we said that England were going to win every game because they are brilliant, it would just not ring true. It's battle-scarred optimism, which is something quite modest and very English and I think people can relate to that a lot more.'

After opening with vocal samples of television pundits Trevor Brooking and Alan Hansen decrying the awful state of English football, the song moves on to more positive lyrical territory and finishes on a heartfelt but uplifting note. The plaintive refrain with which it begins – '*it's coming home, it's coming home, it's coming, football's coming home*' – had its origins in the official *Euro 96* tournament slogan, Football Comes Home. The phrase had struck in the mind of Broudie on account of its presence on the pennants which hung from the lamp posts that lined Edge Lane and some of the other main approach roads into Liverpool – one of the tournament's major venue cities – during the run-in to the competition. It was a perfect fit for a melody line that the Lightning Seeds had been messing around with for months. The band were in the throes of making their fourth album, *Dizzy Heights*, but had already recorded more than enough uptempo, on-the-beat pop numbers. Broudie knew that this particular tune, which originally had a strong Beach Boys harmonic flavour to it, was too good to cast aside. So, when the English Football Association approached the band with a view to recording an England song for the tournament, the track was the obvious one to use.

'The FA asked me to write an England song,' recalls singer and guitarist Broudie. 'But when I sat down to think about it, I came to the conclusion that it was going to be really difficult. People think of pop music and football as being quite close in the 1990s and point to 'World in Motion' as being the perfect meeting between the two cultures. But I still thought it was going to be really difficult. There hadn't been a football record in ages that was a football song *and* a fan's anthem. There had been bad ones, of course, but not many good ones. We could have sidestepped the issue and done something that was basically an advert, got one or two of the players to rap over some beats. But that would have been avoiding the issue. I wanted to do make a football song and make it good. I wanted it to be a football song that meant something. I really liked 'World in Motion'. It was a perfect song for *Italia 90*, but it wasn't a song about football, so I didn't want to do a repeat of 'World in Motion'.

'I wanted words that England fans could relate to, which is why I had the idea of asking Frank and David to write the lyrics. I wanted them to be realistic. I didn't want it to say that we were going to win everything in sight. I wanted it to be a song for supporters who had stood in the rain and watched their team. At first, I didn't want the team to sing on it at all. Then, after realising that I was going to have a couple of stand-up comics singing on it, that didn't seem to matter so much. So we ignored those factors and just set their lyrics to my melody. The minute we put the two together, I knew it was going to work.

'When it was first released, 'Three Lions' wasn't very well received by the media. It suffered from a 'World in Motion' hangover. People wanted another song in the same style. They probably wanted a song with some rapping on it, exactly the sort of song that I didn't want to do. So, with the exception of *NME*, the critics were initially cool towards the song. Even Radio One weren't particularly supportive of the single at first.'

Baddiel, Skinner and the Lightning Seeds had made a song that they felt the average English football fan could relate to. Even they, though, never really imagined that a packed-to-the-rafters Wembley Stadium would actually unite in full-throated communal renditions of the song during the tournament. The atmosphere at the tournament's opening fixture – a dull drawn game at Wembley between England and Switzerland – was still relatively lacklustre, the subdued mood of the Hungarian match three weeks previously appearing to linger on, despite the much-healthier attendance figure. But, in the week between the opening game and the next England fixture – the eagerly-anticipated domestic spat against ancient rivals Scotland – there were subtle signs that the national mood was starting to change. Even though the England team were vilified by Fleet Street for their showing against Switzerland, *Euro 96* was capturing the public imagination. And 'Three Lions' was clearly part of that process.

The afternoon of the England-Scotland game had begun inauspiciously with the Tartan Army, the travelling armada of Scottish fans, in far more vociferous form than their English counterparts. One familiar refrain in the sun-drenched car parks around Wembley Stadium sought to demonise Jimmy Hill, the BBC's football pundit. Hill was a long-standing figure of fun among Scottish fans for what was viewed as a patronising attitude towards a decent side who had a far better World Cup qualifying record than England during the 1970s. In addition to berating Hill and reminding onlooking England fans that the Scots were now '*the best behaved supporters in the land*', the Tartan Army also appropriated the Monkees' hit 'Daydream Believer'. The song had been rewritten earlier in the season by Sunderland fans celebrating their side's promotion to the Premiership. Rather than salute Roker Park boss Peter Reid, though, the coarser Scottish version sought only to denigrate the home fans, all of whom were deemed '*sad English bastards with a crap football team*'.

Though they occupied a smaller section of seating inside the stadium, the Scottish fans were easily the noisier supporters in a tense, scoreless first half. Whereas the English ranks were looking to their team to lift the crowd, the Scottish contingent sung almost constantly in an effort to lift their team. During the half-time interval, however, something appeared to change among the home supporters. Undoubtedly sparked by the Scottish fans, and aided by the efforts of the resident Wembley DJ Steve Kemsley, the England hordes began to finally find their true voice and 'Three Lions' began to take hold inside the stadium for the first time. It wasn't only one of the defining moments of the tournament, but arguably a defining moment in the history of English football fandom.

Kemsley, a video producer by day, was undoubtedly one of the unsung heroes of *Euro 96*. As well as announcing the teams over the stadium Tannoy, he played CDs before the game, at half-time and after the final whistle. Among his favourites at *Euro 96* were 'We Will Rock You' by Queen, 'Sit Down' by James, 'Walking on Sunshine' by Katrina and the Waves and 'Shake a Tail Feather' by the Blues Brothers. In an attempt to remain non-partisan in the pre-match build-up to England-Scotland, he had alternated 'Three Lions' with Rod Stewart's official Scotland record. During the half-time interval of this so-called Battle of Britain, he also played an old rock 'n' roll instrumental, 'Tequila' by the Champs. The latter drink was the spirit that members of the England squad had been pictured consuming in the 'dentist's chair', to massive tabloid outrage, on their pre-tournament visit to Hong Kong. But while the DJ's waspish gesture passed largely unnoticed by the Wembley hordes, his half-time airing of 'Three Lions' didn't. Faced with being outsung once again on home turf by the Tartan Army, the England fans took up the '*it's coming home*' refrain and never let it go.

'The turning point for England, both on and off the field, was the Scotland game,' Kemsley told me later. 'The Scotland supporters were simply magnificent during the half-time interval and their passion eventually stirred something in the English. For the first time in the tournament, they really began singing the song. And things snowballed from there, with the flag waving, a brass band at the next match and a genuine improvement in the atmosphere at the games.'

Inspired partly by the home supporters finally getting behind them and partly by the shrewd introduction of midfielder Jamie Redknapp in the second half, England eventually overcame the Scots to win 2-0. With Alan Shearer scoring the first and David Seaman saving a Gary McAllister penalty, it was left to Paul Gascoigne – booed throughout by the Scottish fans – to put a quiet first-half behind him and seal the points for England with a wonderful individual goal.

It had been a long time in coming, but England and their fans finally had a long-overdue moment of genuine Wembley glory to savour. The victory was understandably milked after the final whistle. Even though the FA had cautioned him against it, Kemsley played 'Three Lions' – along with the Scotland song – once again. As he did so, the stadium erupted with a spontaneity unheard since 1966. As the bald-headed Steve Stone, a second-half England substitute, danced on the Wembley pitch in much the same manner as Nobby Stiles had '*thirty years of hurt*' ago, Skinner and Baddiel moved to the railings near the Royal Box. The pair then led the communal singing from the stand beneath the Twin Towers, Skinner kissing the three lions on his replica shirt before Baddiel turned round to the DJ box to thank Kemsley for 'the best three minutes of my life'.

But the colourful Wembley scenes, for which the Scottish fans must still take the initial credit, were just the start. A song that supported England without being particularly jingoistic, 'Three Lions' was soon heard from fans during matches in which England weren't even playing. According to Steve Beauchampe, an organiser of the 'fan embassies' set up for *Euro 96* by the Football Supporters Association, it was the England-Scotland game that set a musical and cultural spectacle in motion. 'That was the game that started it,' he recalls. 'It was the point that a lot of people suddenly realised how much they liked 'Three Lions'. It was the eighth or ninth game in the tournament and I still remember everyone getting into it at half-time. It was an amazing moment.'

It was at the England-Scotland game, too, that the first of many 'Three Lions' variations was sung, the England fans taunting their beaten but unbowed Scottish counterparts with the refrain '*you're going home, you're going home*' all along Olympic Way at the end of the match.

What had started as a surf-style melody knocked around a rehearsal room by the Lightning Seeds had turned into a people's anthem in the space of a few weeks. The manner in which 'Three Lions' was sung at subsequent England matches at Wembley – with even the Spanish and German supporters adopting it in the quarter-final and semi-final respectively – was a throwback to an era when the foundations of the nation's football stadia regularly shook to the collective choruses of fans singing up for their team. There had, of course, been singing at England matches in the past, but never to such a degree. The phenomenon was, for the more optimistic, a pointer towards a future in which England supporters could offer intense vocal backing to their team without resorting to jingoism and racism. For those fortunate enough to be at Wembley in June 1996 to watch England, it certainly seemed as if a musical and cultural watershed had been reached.

'Three Lions' had gone straight into the UK singles chart at number one in the week of release. After slipping down in subsequent weeks, the record returned to the top of the chart as *Euro 96* progressed and it became increasingly entwined with the fortunes of an England side which was winning vital matches and also playing with a degree of flair and tactical nous that surprised its many detractors. Ironically, as a song which studiously avoided the triumphant tone of past efforts, the lyric-ally-modest 'Three Lions' was associated with an English success story on the field.

'You have to remember that before *Euro 96*, England hadn't played a meaningful, competitive match since the reign of Graham Taylor,' says Ian Broudie. 'Even though the team of Terry Venables had looked okay in the warm-up games, it was anyone's guess as to how we would do in a proper tournament. There was always a chance that England were going to be absolutely awful, so we had to have a song that took account of that possibility. But, when the Wembley crowd started singing it dur-ing the England-Scotland game, that was it. It suddenly felt as if we had done it. We had made a proper football song. From that point onwards, the song went out of our domain and became public property.'

The song – which had become virtually an alternative national anthem by the time England played Germany in the semi-final – was also vital in motivating the England team. 'It caught everyone's imagination,' Steve McManaman, the Liverpool and England winger told *NME* a year later. 'By the time we got to the Germany game, we had people lining the route all the way from Bisham Abbey to Wembley and I think it was that song that did it. Before every game, we'd listen to a tape of the single on the coach as we approached Wembley. One day we lost the tape and the coach had already arrived in the tunnel. We had to stay on the coach until we found it and played it. It was part of the pre-match ritual.'

While the *Euro 96* showdown with Germany ended in defeat via the most narrow of margins – the inevitable penalty shoot-out – the song outlived the tournament. It was sung as '*fussball's coming home*' by the German squad, led by captain Jürgen Klinsmann, on their victorious return to home base in Frankfurt on the Monday after their final tri-umph over the Czech Republic, and went on to become a massive hit in Germany. It has become a staple at all England home games and witty variations on the refrain '*it's coming home*' have been adapted countless times at club level.

For Ian Broudie, the former Liverpool punk thrust into the glare of the mainstream partially on the back of a football song, the success of 'Three Lions' was gratifying. It hadn't been a corny cash-in like some of the football anthems of the past. It had been penned and played on his terms. Fingering the mood of the British people with far more accura-cy than the tabloid newspapers – which had tried to whip up an ill-judged frenzy of xenophobia before the matches against Spain and Germany – the song helped to define a refreshing, more outward-looking national mood. It was a classic case of the counter culture – indie pop and alternative comedy – infiltrating the mainstream and pulling off a stylish and significant away win.

'When I was playing in punk bands in the late 1970s, the prospect of doing a football song was about as unlikely as things could get,' Broudie says. 'But, after seeing what happened with 'Three Lions', I felt as if the world had moved to me. But that's often the way of it. Things begin by being left-field and ultimately end up being in the mainstream. With 'Three Lions', though, I feel as if the mainstream moved to me rather than vice versa. It was strange, but it didn't seem out of place to be doing a football song, even one that became so widespread during the summer of 1996. It was one of those rare moments where you set out to do something and it just fits in perfectly with the mood of the time.'

VICTORY OR DEATH!

I t would be absurd to pinpoint a precise moment in time when football witnessed its first bout of crowd chanting. Songs of encouragement and screams of condemnation from the sidelines have been part of the game ever since the Football Association was formed and its original set of rules drafted by a group of former public schoolboys in a London pub in 1863. With the introduction of the FA Cup eight years later, formally competitive football began to replace relaxed friendlies and supporters started to flock to matches in significant numbers. In November 1872, over four thousand spectators, paying a shilling apiece, watched the first ever international football match in the grounds of the West Of Scotland Cricket Club in Partick, Glasgow. The game, between Scotland and England, finished in a goalless draw. It can probably be assumed that the forerunners of the Tartan Army generated far more noise than any travelling English fans who happened to be at the game.

As football grew in sophistication in the later years of the Nineteenth Century – with the advent of goal-nets, the crossbar, a referee's whistle, shinpads and the two-handed throw-in – so crowd figures gradually increased. The introduction of half-day working on Saturdays in the 1870s allowed large numbers of factory employees the luxury of watching football in the afternoon. A great British tradition, one which also involved the inevitable pre-match pub lunch, was taking shape.

The earliest black and white photograph of a football match shows sections of a flat-capped crowd of 15,000 watching the 1887 FA Cup Final between Aston Villa and West Bromwich Albion at The Oval in Kennington, South London. With the national rail network expanding, the practice of supporters travelling to away matches, particularly cup ties, grew rapidly in the late Nineteenth Century. Blackburn Olympic, the first northern side to dent the supremacy of the southern public schools in the FA Cup, beat Old Etonians in the 1883 final at The Oval and returned home to a chaotic reception. Parading the trophy through the Lancashire mill town, the team were greeted by ecstatic fans, one of whom supposedly bellowed to team captain Alf Warburton: 'Look at t'Cup, it's like a copper kettle. Still, it's welcome here, and it'll never go back to London.'

By the end of the century, following the formation of the English, Scottish and Irish leagues, football's popularity had soared to such an extent that the FA were seeking out bigger venues for their prestigious final tie. In the 1894 final, which featured Notts County and Bolton Wanderers, the action took place before 37,000 fans at Goodison Park, home of Everton. By 1901, it had been switched to Crystal Palace in South London, where 115,000 fans saw eventual winners Tottenham Hotspur – then without the questionable benefits of a 'rockney' Cup Final song recorded with Chas And Dave – take on Sheffield United.

Though there is little evidence of concentrated singing in unison on the terraces during football's formative years, there were specific songs that grew to be affiliated with certain clubs. The traditional Geordie anthem 'Blaydon Races', which commemorated horse racing at a course south of the River Tyne, was composed by local writer George Ridley in 1862 and has been associated with Newcastle United for a number of years. Still heard long before kick-off in the pubs, such as The Strawberry and The Trent House, near St James's Park, the song took off in the early Fifties, coinciding with Newcastle's FA Cup wins of 1951, 1952 and 1955. The Norwich City anthem 'On The Ball City' also dates from the late Nineteenth Century. Though originally written for another local club, it has been linked with the Canaries ever since their formation in 1902.

The early part of the Twentieth Century saw the worldwide spread of football, although the British associations remained sniffily aloof of developments across the globe. None of the home countries sent a team to the first ever World Cup, held in Uruguay in 1930, and Britain remained indifferent to the tournament until after the Second World War. In terms of the history of football supporters, the 1930 World Cup was notable for the astonishing scenes that preceded the Final. Held in the Uruguayan capital of Montevideo, it pitched the home side against Argentina, their traditional arch rivals from just across the River Plate. On the eve of the match, large numbers of Argentinians crossed the short stretch of water accompanied by the chilling battle cry of 'victory or death!'. In the event, the Final passed off relatively peacefully, despite a 4-2 win for the home team in front of 90,000 frenzied fans, many of whom had been searched for pistols and other weapons beforehand.

Though it was developing in isolation from the rest of the world, support for the game in Britain continued to grow in the first half of the Twentieth Century. A crowd estimated at 250,000, many of whom had scaled the stadium walls to get in, attended the first FA Cup Final to be played at Wembley, between Bolton Wanderers and West Ham United, in 1923. In Scotland, too, the game's popularity rocketed and a *Glasgow Observer* account of the 1924 Old Firm derby between Glasgow Rangers and Celtic at Ibrox spoke of the 'thunderous chants and rousing choruses' that rained down from the terraces during the match.

With little else to divert the population from the harsh realities of rationing and austerity after the Second World War, the late Forties saw a dramatic, euphoric peak in attendance figures at football grounds. As the economic restrictions of the post-war years eased, however, with the leisure choices available to the masses increasing, the massive gates of the Forties tailed off slightly.

But, while ordinary working people were starting to invest in television sets and motor cars during the Fifties, the Saturday afternoon match ritual remained a vital ingredient in the lives of many. The Fifties saw the most pronounced flowering to date of football songs and chants. When Portsmouth won the First Division title for two consecutive seasons in 1949 and 1950, their triumph was notable not only for the fact that their team was largely recruited from servicemen stationed on the south coast during the war, but also for the aural accompaniment of the so-called 'Pompey Chimes'. Based on the ding-dong of a chiming clock, the chant consisted of the simple refrain '*play up Pompey, Pompey play up*'.

Another crucial song from the same period is the Birmingham City anthem 'Keep Right On' or, to give the tune its proper name, 'The End Of The Road'. Written and first recorded by the long-deceased Scottish singer Sir Harry Lauder, it became popular with Blues players and fans during the team's run to the 1956 FA Cup Final. Introduced by Scottish player Alex Govan, the song was sung by the team on their train journeys to important cup ties and was soon taken up by supporters. The song did not bring the City side much luck at Wembley, however, where they were beaten 3-1 by Manchester City. As communal terrace chanting became more prevalent in the early Sixties, however, the song was also taken up by fans of Manchester United and Tottenham Hotspur. But it remains a number that will always be most strongly linked with the club which first sang it.

Tim Ross, sports editor of 1152 Xtra AM in Birmingham, recalled what 'The End Of The Road' still means to Blues fans in the sleeve notes for a compilation CD of City songs released in 1997 on the Cherry Red label: 'Like many other supporters, I first heard it sitting on my dad's knee. And, from that day on, the hairs have stood on the back of my neck every time I hear it. It is still the first song that any Blues fan learns, and the story of how it became an anthem is legendary in Birmingham. Alex Govan is owed a debt by all Blues fans. Every time I see him, he starts singing it.'

While songs were becoming an ever intensifying part of football in the late Fifties, the sounds of the terraces still consisted more of loud cheers, barked insults and ribald banter than full-blown choral eruptions. Britain was slowly emerging from its austere post-war slumber, but a general air of formality, restraint and public decorum remained. At the same time, however, the rise of rock 'n' roll music – teddy boys, inner city gangs and the slashing of urban cinema seats – was accompanied by the first stirrings of football violence. Initially, this occurred well away from the stadia, the trains which carried fans to games often ending up with their windows broken and their seats slashed as the first generation of juvenile delinquents went on the rampage.

As the Fifties drew to a close, the game approached a watershed that would have repercussions into the next decade and way beyond. Football was changing. And the sounds of the terraces were about to blossom into what was undoubtedly their golden age. The changes on the terraces between the twilight zone of the late Fifties and the new dawn of the Sixties were summed up by writer Arthur Hopcraft in his 1968 book *The Football Man*.

In his book, Hopcraft contrasted the rehearsed, disciplined chants which arose in the Sixties with the 'lone, amazing voices' he remembered hearing when he watched Wolverhampton Wanderers in his youth. The old-fashioned terrace catcalls were inspired by the wit and spontaneity of the workplace and usually took the form of insults that were directed at individuals on the field of play, such as the winger who 'couldn't run a raffle' or the reticent linesman who needed help in raising what was obviously a very heavy flag. The unison chanting that emerged in the Sixties, on the other hand, was more like a 'plainsong' of the terraces.

The full flowering of the football anthem coincided with the pop boom of the early Sixties. The common consensus is that the singing really began in earnest on Merseyside and, particularly, on the legendary Spion Kop at Anfield. But, while the Kop Choir remain football's most celebrated terrace tunesmiths, there is evidence to suggest that South American fans also had a role in starting the chanting of the Sixties.

In May 1959, an England side under the guidance of Walter Winterbottom completed a disastrous three-match tour of South America, in which they were beaten by Brazil, Peru and Mexico. The game against World Cup holders Brazil in Rio De Janiero – which the home side won 2-0 with goals by Julinho and Henrique – was shown on television in Britain. The match not only exposed the increasingly-clear technical limitations of the British game. It also exposed British viewers to the hypnotic shouts of the ardent Brazilian fans for the first time.

The most fundamental Brazilian chant of the late Fifties involved a constant repetition of the phrase '*Bra-sil, cha-cha-cha! Bra-sil, cha-cha-cha!*'. A few months later, at the start of the 1959-60 season, variations of the Brazilian mantra began to appear at British league grounds. At first, supporters copied the South American style exactly, following the name of their own team with a series of '*cha-cha-chas*'. Eventually, the '*cha-cha-chas*' developed into stacatto handclaps and it was this later modification which provided the backing track to England's victory in the 1966 World Cup at Wembley.

As the familiar clatter of the football rattle began to fade during the early Sixties, the '*cha-cha-chas*' were augmented by other chants that had more of a playground flavour to them. Skipping rhymes such as '*two-four-six-eight, who do we appreciate?*' started to become commonplace. In addition to exclamations of support, the burgeoning rowdy element also took to insulting the opposing team with taunts such as 'Rovers – Bugger off!' or 'United – Under the arm!', the latter jibe referring to a part of the human anatomy which was deemed unpleasant. Such insults might appear tame these days, but were considered vulgar in the wildly different moral climate of the late Fifties and early Sixties.

But, with the adoption and adaptation of pop music, the sounds of the supporters began taking on new dimensions. Nowhere was this more conspicuous than on the Kop, the massive standing-only terrace that still occupies a unique place in British footballing folklore. Named after the site of a bloody battle in the South African Boer War, the earliest Kop terrace was built in 1906. After the original mound had been concreted over, the stand was given a roof – then the largest single span structure assembled at a football ground – in 1928. But it was in the early Sixties that the Kop was propelled into the imagination of millions.

It had previously been considered that Welsh international rugby crowds were the most musical in the world. That changed when the Kop burst into song. Inspired partly by the pugnacious humour that is part of the city's character and partly by the emerging strains of the beat boom that was sweeping the port's nightclubs, the 28,000 souls who stood on The Kop started to express themselves with passionate versions of pop hits such as 'She Loves You' by The Beatles, 'I Like It' by Freddie And The Dreamers and 'Anyone Who Had A Heart' by Cilla Black. 'You'll Never Walk Alone', the song that was to become their anthem, was written by Rodgers and Hammerstein for the musical Carousel, but adopted by the Kop after Gerry And The Pacemakers charted with the track in 1963.

It was a boom time on Merseyside. The docks were thriving, light entertainers such as Jimmy Tarbuck and Ken Dodd were breaking into showbusiness and The Beatles were changing the face of pop. The optimism within the city was reflected by the buoyancy of the Kop, a swirling mass of humanity which was usually worth at least a one-goal start to Liverpool at Anfield. Liverpool manager Bill Shankly was quick to pay tribute to the effect the Kop had on his team – and the demoralising impact they would sometimes have on the opposition. Shankly, who occasionally stood on the terrace himself to savour its unique spirit, regularly praised the Koppites. When a recording of the Kop Choir in full voice was released on vinyl in the Sixties, it was Shankly who penned the sleeve notes.

'The Kop are unique,' wrote Shankly. 'They are fair, humorous, well behaved and well educated on the game. They love to see good football being played and if a team comes to Anfield and uses any foul methods, the Kop will be on them like a shot. But if a team comes and plays well, they will be applauded almost as if they were the home team. The Kop have a great sense of humour, although it can sometimes be cruel. Like the time when Liverpool were playing Leeds. Their goalkeeper, Gary Sprake, picked the ball up at one stage and pulled his arm back to throw it out, but it span out of his hand and into the goal. Immediately, the Kop began to sing 'Careless Hands' which, although it seemed a bit hard on poor Gary at the time, illustrates how quickly they react.'

Though there is definite truth in Shankly's words about the fairness of the Kop, the intimidatory effect they could have on visiting sides was huge, often with refrains far more savage than the Des O'Connor song that Sprake had to contend with. Defenders knew that they could ill afford to be indiscreet in the penalty area. The Kop were renowned for an ability to appeal in unison for a foul that would result in a Liverpool penalty. Even in the Eighties, visiting players were regularly subjected to the infamous Anfield factor, as former Tottenham Hotspur striker Garth Crooks explained in *The Sunday Times Illustrated History of Football* in 1995. Crooks, who scored the solitary goal which gave Spurs a famous away win against Liverpool in March 1985, asserted that The Kop used humour as a 'satirical sword' to psyche out the opposition: 'Before you even got to the generals of Anfield, you had to deal with the infantry'.

Such was the reputation of the Kop in the Sixties that BBC's *Panorama* dispatched an outside broadcast unit to Anfield to watch Liverpool thrash Arsenal 5-0 and clinch the 1963-64 First Division title. The bewildered voiceover that accompanied the story reported that the behaviour of the Kop was unlike that of any other football crowd. It spoke of the strong links between Merseybeat and the songs of the Liverpool fans and went on to compare the richness of terrace life with the mysteries that an anthropologist might encounter on a South Sea island. The film makers, however, were most staggered by the degree to which the performance was an organised ritual, with the crowd appearing to sing new songs with one, huge voice.

As the Kop's fame started to spread, other teams started to imitate the sound, even though few could match either the volume or humour of the Liverpudlians in the Sixties. As well as pop numbers and traditional songs, television adverts became a source of terrace chants. An example was the slogan '*HP Baked Beans – they're the ones for me*' which was transformed into '*Port Vale FC – they're the team for me*'.

Violence, however, was also on the rise. In the Sixties, the aggression moved out of the railway carriages and into the streets between the train stations and the stadia. Eventually, the fighting shifted into the football grounds themselves, as gangs affiliated with one club began to seek out the supporters of their rivals. Outbreaks of stadium warfare were routinely accompanied by chants and songs which derided and threatened the opposition as well as boasting of previous triumphs on the terraces. The Chris Montez hit 'Let's Dance', inevitably, was mutated into 'Let's Fight'. The trouble tended to be focussed on the vast standing areas behind the goals, the so-called 'ends', in which territory was gained or conceded as if contested by two clashing medieval armies.

Regarded with disdain by the police, clubs and transport officials alike, the terrace hoodlums changed their sartorial styles with successive generations. Sixties skinheads became the smooths and suedeheads of the Seventies and the casuals, scallies and baggies of the Eighties. But their songs remained essentially the same, focusing on basic themes of defending their honour and their 'manor' and giving any opposing fans a chasing.

The violence was often unsavoury and – particularly as the use of knives intensified in the Seventies and Eighties – often quite sickening. But the perpetrators were also invariably among their chosen club's most loyal and vociferous travelling supporters. The attitude of a Tottenham fan interviewed on the train journey to an away match in the Hunter Davies book *The Glory Game* was typical of the early Seventies: 'The club call us hooligans, but who'd cheer them on if we didn't come? You have to stand there and take it when Spurs are losing and the others are jeering at you. It's not easy. We support them everywhere, but we get no thanks.'

Despite the terrace rucks and rumbles, players and managers knew that there would be no game without the supporters. Danny Blanchflower, the articulate Tottenham captain from an earlier and more Corinthian era, had put it perfectly during the Sixties: 'The noise of the crowd, the singing and the chanting, is the oxygen we players breathe.'

Decades later, when English supporters were again being admonished in the wake of trouble at the 1992 European Championship in Sweden, another big football name would spring to their defence. Eric Cantona, then with Leeds United, claimed that the loyalty of the English fan stood in contrast with the attitude of football followers in his native France. 'English fans are brilliant,' said Cantona. 'In England, when you ask someone which club he supports, it means something. The guy supports a club for the whole of his life, whatever the ups and downs. In France, there's no loyalty. If you're not top of the league, the fans go to another club.'

In the Sixties, Seventies and Eighties, certain songs became associated with particular crowds. Just as Liverpool fans had 'You'll Never Walk Alone' and Newcastle 'The Blaydon Races', so the supporters of other clubs seized on a pop hit or traditional song and made it their signature tune, often without making any changes to the lyrical content.

Elvis never left the building as far as fans of Port Vale, Sunderland or Manchester City were concerned, the three clubs respectively adopting Presley's vintage hits 'The Wonder Of You', 'Can't Help Falling In Love' and 'Blue Moon'. The latter is the subject of some dispute, however, with Crewe fans – despite the fact that their team play in red – claiming to have been the first to sing it. Burslem club Port Vale's adoption of 'The Wonder Of You' has regularly been taken to extreme lengths by supporters, up to 500 of whom have dressed up in the full rhinestone regalia of Presley's Las Vegas years when travelling to away matches at Christmas and at the end of the season.

Among other identifiable team songs are 'Glad All Over' by the Dave Clark Five at Crystal Palace, 'Goodnight Irene' by Leadbelly at Bristol Rovers, 'The Eton Boating Song' at Coventry, 'I've Got A Lovely Bunch Of Coconuts' at Cambridge United', 'The Liquidator' by Harry J All Stars at West Bromwich Albion and Wolves, 'Hi Ho Silver Lining' by Jeff Beck at Sheffield Wednesday, 'Annie's Song' by John Denver at Sheffield United, 'Love Is In The Air' by John Paul Young at Dundee United, 'Delilah' by either Tom Jones or The Sensational Alex Harvey Band at Stoke City and, of course, 'I'm Forever Blowing Bubbles' at West Ham. The latter was first played over the Tannoy at the Boleyn Ground in the Twenties.

With each new pop movement, fresh material was introduced. The Seventies were a particularly fruitful decade as singles such as 'Sailing' by Rod Stewart, 'Amazing Grace' by Judy Collins, 'Son Of My Father' by Chicory Tip, 'My Friend Stan' by Slade, 'Oh Boy' by Mud, 'Longlegged Woman Dressed In Black' by Mungo Jerry, 'Seasons In The Sun' by Terry

Jacks and even Clive Dunn's novelty Christmas hit 'Grandad' all forced their way onto the terraces in some form. One of the more quirky songs of this era to make an impact was the Johnny Mathis ballad 'When A Child Is Born', the tune of which was simply hummed in unison by thousands of fans. Many of the tunes from this period remained a strong part of a typical terrace set-list well into the Nineties. With pop's artistic decline during the Eighties, however, fewer songs made an enduring transition from the charts to the terraces. One of the few Eighties songs to have had a lasting impact was not even a pop number at all, but the Caribbean carnival anthem 'Hot, Hot, Hot'. Originally recorded by soca star Arrow, it became particularly well entrenched at Highbury, where Arsenal fans replaced the song's *'Feeling hot, hot, hot'* hook with the *'Ian Wright, Wright, Wright'* refrain.

Of the punk and post-punk songs of the late Seventies and Eighties, only a few found their way into football. Liverpool fans sang 'Down In The Tube Station At Midnight' by The Jam and 'The English Civil War' by The Clash, the latter a punk version of the American battle anthem 'When Johnny Comes Marching Home'. The Kop also briefly adopted the chorus of another Clash song, 'The Call Up', during a title-clinching win over Tottenham in May 1992, a match played during the Falklands War.

The Eighties, for all the European trophies won by Liverpool, Nottingham Forest, Aston Villa, Everton and Tottenham, were a grim decade for English football. The disasters at Bradford, Heysel and Hillsborough cast a tragic shadow over the game. Serious crowd trouble at home and abroad – in particular at an FA Cup Sixth Round tie between Luton Town and Millwall in 1985 – encouraged the Tory government to start planning a national identity card scheme for football fans, threatening to impose a levy on transfer fees to pay for the project. It was only after Lord Justice Taylor – in his 1990 report into the Hillsborough disaster – declared that identity cards were potentially dangerous due to the congestion they could cause outside grounds, that the government dropped the scheme.

But, with football under siege from an unsympathetic government, there was some light relief to be had on the terraces in the 1988-89 season. A craze for plastic inflatables was instigated by the banana-wielding fans of Manchester City. The gesture was an ironic tribute to City striker Imre Varadi, whose surname, incongruously, was deemed to rhyme with banana. The fad quickly spread, other notable manifestations being the inevitable canaries at Norwich, spotted dogs at Oldham Athletic, turtles at Stockport County and a shoal of fish, all called Harry The Haddock, that surfaced during Grimsby Town's FA Cup run.

The most absurd terrace anthem of the Eighties and early Nineties was 'The Celery Song', which suggested the possibility of sexual gratification via the strategic application of a certain household vegetable. The song is thought to have originated at Brighton's Goldstone Ground before spreading to Gillingham and Bournemouth. But it was at Stamford Bridge where the song attained most volume, usually accompanied by the tossing into the air of sticks of celery and sweetcorn. As Chelsea faced Manchester United in the 1993-94 FA Cup Final, the most bizarre sight on Olympic Way was the spectacle of otherwise ordinary people walking around with vegetables sticking out of their top pockets. It was a fashion which left the Manchester United winger Ryan Giggs bemused: 'When I took a free kick near the Chelsea fans, they started chucking things at me. Nothing unusual there, except that it wasn't the usual plastic cups or cans. It was sticks of celery. I don't know what it was all about, but it made me laugh to think of them popping into the grocer's shops on the way to Wembley.'

To Scottish winger Pat Nevin, ex-chairman of the English Professional Footballers Association, surrealist crazes such as inflatables and celery represented football fans reclaiming the game: 'Taken in isolation, they were daft spectacles. But, in retrospect, I think they were important. It was a case of the fans stealing football back from the thugs. Inflatables were part of that. They signified a change of mood that culminated in the relatively good behaviour of England fans during *Euro 96*.'

In the aftermath of the Taylor Report, the football grounds of Britain are now far safer places for supporters. The facilities at most Premiership and First Division clubs are of a standard befitting the national sport. But, with the removal of terraces and the arrival of all-seater stadia, the nature of the singing at football matches has changed. Many fans believe the huge tidal waves of chanting in unison are now a thing of the past. It is claimed that the creeping gentrification of the game has cut football adrift from its working class roots. With more sections of football grounds being given over to expensive seating, executive boxes and family areas, the intensity of the singing has diminished. Or so the argument goes.

But while the game has changed, putting blame on the Taylor Report, which recommended the installation of all-seater stadia in the top two divisions, is irresponsible and simplistic. It was surely vital that the lessons of Hillsborough were learnt and put into practice. Besides, there are other factors – high prices, officious stewarding, restrictions on away fans and the spread of satellite television – that have contributed to the changed atmosphere in British football grounds. The sheer cost of going to matches has certainly driven some supporters away. When Liverpool played Aston Villa in the Semi-Final of the 1995-96 FA Cup at Old Trafford, the crowd figure was more than 10,000 below the ground's capacity at the time and whole rows of seats were left empty.

And, despite all the gloomy prognostications, the singing does go on. The Nineties, arguably a much better decade for pop than the Eighties, have seen a plethora of new chants emerge and take hold across the country. When the Pet Shop Boys revived the classic disco hit 'Go West' in 1993, the last thing on their minds was the creation of a new football anthem. But the song, originally a hit for the Village People in 1979, was quickly adopted by fans. There are suggestions that the track was first sung by football fans in the German Bundesliga, though the refrain 'Go West, Bromwich Albion' was also one early example of the song's popularity. A booming soundtrack to Arsenal's single-goal victory over Parma in Copenhagen in the 1994 European Cup-Winners' Cup Final – 'One-nil to the Arsenal' – it has since cropped up in countless other guises.

While the chanting might not boast the awesome intensity that a full house could muster in the era of packed terraces, the songs are more prevalent globally in the Nineties. Many overseas fans now adopt the chants of their British counterparts and have devised others of their own. As well as introducing 'Go West', Euro-fans pioneered the ubiquitous 'ole, ole, ole, ole' refrain, while Dutch fans were behind a popular chant based on the hit 'No Limit' by 2 Unlimited. Fans of the Andalucian clubs of southern Spain such as Real Betis and Sevilla FC, meanwhile, specialise in rhythmic clapping reminiscent of the cadences of local flamenco beats.

The rise of Britpop in the early Nineties gave more inspiration to football's choristers. Maine Road regulars were supplied with an unforgettable anthem in 'Wonderwall' by fellow Manchester City fans Oasis while 'Don't Look Back In Anger' and 'Stand By Me' have also been aired. Then there were official team songs such as England's 'Three Lions', Chelsea's 'Blue Day' and Sunderland's version of the Monkees hit 'Daydream Believer', all sung with passion and fervour. And, with the more eclectic pop of the late Nineties retaining much of Britpop's classic melodicism, there should still be enough new raw material for the chants to keep developing well into the next millennium.

KICKER CONSPIRACIES

During the late 1970s and early 1980s, it was impossible to imagine football and music ever operating in the same cultural domain. The two activities had flirted with one another during the Swinging Sixties, when George Best of Manchester United was dubbed 'El Beatle' and the Kop at Anfield used to air word-perfect versions of popular Merseybeat tunes. But by the Seventies – with the exception of the occasional tuneless Cup Final single and the claim of former Brentford trialist and Scotland fan Rod Stewart that football was better than sex – the two pastimes appeared mutually exclusive. It was unthinkable, or certainly unlikely, that you would be into both. When John Peel, DJ and Liverpool supporter, attempted to read out the football scores on Saturday afternoon at the Reading Festival in the Seventies, he would be roundly barracked by Barclay James Harvest fans. Even the punk movement of 1976 was dismissive of football supporters, regarding them with the same distrust that it harboured for disciples of disco music.

The turnaround since those days has been astonishing. Football in the Nineties has moved much closer to pop. The game is marketed and sold with the help of music, the so-called Spice Boy players of Manchester United and Liverpool date female pop stars and Cup Final singles now incorporate the melodies of Britpop or the rhythms of jungle, rap and house. Rock groups now play prestigious shows at their local football grounds, as Oasis did at Maine Road and The Wonderstuff at Walsall's Bescot Stadium. Britpop's culture of Sixties nostalgia is reflected in football's booming market for retro shirts and old match programmes. Damon Albarn, Blur singer and Chelsea fan, can declare that "football is a way of life" while Cure singer Robert Smith can claim the he would "rather be a footballer than an existentialist" and not be ridiculed. And John Peel now gets barracked at the Reading Festival if he *refuses* to read out the football results in full on Saturday afternoon.

In the public euphoria that followed the success of the England team in reaching the Semi-Final of the World Cup in 1990, it was often said that football was "the new rock 'n' roll". For many armchair supporters, their imaginations stoked on a heady diet of Gazza's tears and Pavarotti's operatic tones, football suddenly became fashionable again in the summer of 1990. The legacy of the Eighties – when the establishment had practically declared war on football fans with identity card proposals – was banished practically overnight. With 'World In Motion' supplying the theme tune, soccer allegedly regained the style that had been missing since the Sixties. The game's fashionability soared. Football clubs, sportswear companies and television stations were suddenly making heavy use of pop to promote the sport. But the origins of the bond between the two cultures in the Nineties was not wholly rooted in the populist explosion that followed the 1990 World Cup. Its foundations lay in the terrace fashions and cult music scene of the mid and late Eighties.

In many respects, the Eighties were a grim period for British football. The disasters at Bradford, Heysel and Hillsborough were the lowest points in a decade that was also marred by serious hooliganism, poor facilities in grounds, the continuing failure of the home nations at international level and a drift on the pitch towards brutish athleticism over nimble flair.

The 1980s, however, were also an era of football fanzines and the rise of an alternative terrace culture. It was the decade of wingers such as England's John Barnes and Scotland's Pat Nevin, both as bright and articulate off the field as they were skilful and stylish on it. The 1980s, too, saw the terraces dragged out of the sartorial wilderness as designer clothes took hold. The popularity of brand labels such as Fila, Kappa, Lacoste, Tachinni and Ellesse would later, in the early 1990s, provide a basis for the dress styles of Britpop bands. With terrace chic constantly changing to incorporate a bizarre range of fashions, the tracksuits and rugged outdoor wear which prevailed in the middle of the decade evolved into the scruffier look of the late 1980s that echoed the baggy styles of Manchester bands such as The Stone Roses and Happy Mondays.

The 1980s were also the decade that saw the alternative music scene embrace football through acts such as The Wedding Present, The Fall, Billy Bragg, James, Half Man Half Biscuit, Serious Drinking, Colourbox, The Proclaimers, Tackhead and The Barmy Army. The coming together of football and music – a cornerstone of the game's fashionability in the 1990s – began on the fringes of the early 1980s pop scene. Prior to 1980, music and football had appeared to be two distant and totally unrelated pastimes. Even bands such as The Jam and Madness, both with a strong 'laddish' element to their following, had no obvious connections with the game. Madness singer Suggs, then a regular at Stamford Bridge, even felt compelled to keep his passion for football to himself when Madness emerged in 1979. Almost two decades later, he was to be the vocalist on Chelsea's FA Cup Final single.

'Football was very unhip in the late 1970s,' says Suggs now. 'When Madness first started, I was almost embarrassed to admit that I went to football. The Sex Pistols and The Clash had nothing to do with football. If you saw the occasional punk at a game, he'd always look out of place. Football grounds were not the places for the hip and trendy to be seen. The 1970s were so different to the 1990s. There were some West Ham skinheads and mods who followed bands like Secret Affair and The Cockney Rejects in 1979, but Madness never traded under a football banner. I used to watch Chelsea, but Madness were never a football group. And I wouldn't have dreamed of doing a football song in those days.'

It may have been The Undertones who got the ball rolling with their lyrical references to the table soccer game Subbuteo on 'My Perfect Cousin' in 1980. It might have been Manchester's Ed Banger with 'Kinnel Tommy' or even Serious Drinking with 'Love On The Terraces' and 'Bobby Moore Is Innocent', two anthems which later appeared on the album Stranger Than Tannadice. Or maybe it was Liverpool group Half Man Half Biscuit, who recorded such epics as 'All I Want For Xmas Is A Dukla Prague Away Kit', 'I Was A Teenage Armchair Honved Supporter' and 'Friday Night And The Gates Are Low', the latter a reference to poorly-supported Tranmere Rovers.

However it began, what started as a trickle had become a torrent by the middle of the decade. The Wedding Present called their debut album *George Best*, Colourbox came up with 'The Official Colourbox World Cup Theme' and Billy Bragg wondered how a female friend could '*lie there and think of England, when you don't even know who's in the team*' on 'Greetings To The New Brunette'. Later examples of what became a distinctive musical sub-genre included 'Joyful Kilmarnock Blues' by The Proclaimers, 'Pat Nevin's Eyes' by The Tractors and 'Kicker Conspiracy' by The Fall, the latter with a video shot at Burnley's Turf Moor ground.

Then there were the efforts of London dance and dub producer Adrian Sherwood, a West Ham fan who pioneered the procedure of cutting up and splicing together football chants and match commentaries and setting the results to high-tech electronic rhythms. Working under the names of Tackhead and The Barmy Army, Sherwood's masterful musical collages included the singles 'Sharp As A Needle' and 'The Game'. But the music-football interface was not just restricted to rock. Reggae and world music were represented through 'The Big Match' by Asher Senator and 'Dynamos Vs Caps, 0-0' and 'Tornados Vs Dynamos, 3-3' by Harare-based group The Real Sounds.

In addition to the groups who sang about the game, there were others who used football as a motif. The Manchester band James – who would later record the excellent 'Goal, Goal, Goal' for the 1994 World Cup – put a picture of former Fulham goalkeeper Tony Macedo on the sleeve of the 'Sit Down' single. Liverpool group 35 Summers created a cult fashion item by printing promotional T-shirts featuring a photo of former Liverpool boss Bill Shankly. And The Housemartins, after calling their debut album *London 0, Hull 4*, printed up tour passes featuring the face of the then Nottingham Forest manager Brian Clough.

One of the great allies of football-affiliated 1980s pop was John Peel, who championed practically all the acts mentioned, his support wavering only on the night his beloved Liverpool won the 1984 European Cup, when he missed the start of his Radio One evening show in order to watch the televised climax of the decisive penalty shoot-out in Rome.

Alternative pop's fixation with football in the 1980s was not the stuff of anorak-wearing musical trainspotters. All the bands mentioned were true football fans. And they had points to make, firstly in railing against a bland and remote pop establishment and secondly in voicing disenchantment with the direction in which football was heading. The fans they attracted, too, included a sizable proportion of hardcore football elements. New Order were the biggest alternative rock band of the 1980s and their live shows in Manchester, Blackburn and Leeds were regularly attended not by the stereotypically fey fans of independent music, but by many of the more vociferous local football supporters.

The 1987 song 'Three English Football Grounds' by the Fall-influenced South London band I Ludicrous was particularly representative of the mood of the time. Taken from the band's debut EP *It's Like Everything Else*, the track was a supporter's guide to Millwall's original Den in Cold Blow Lane, Bolton's Burnden Park and Fulham's Craven Cottage. The lyrics came complete with details of admission prices – which ran from £2.50 to £4.00 – and ratings for the beer. Ten years later, rather tellingly, two of the three grounds mentioned had been demolished and the third, Craven Cottage, had only just survived the bulldozers. Of The Den, the band had sung: '*We are not animals, we are human beings, our supporters loyal. Their enthusiasm only leads to violence as a result of immense provocation.*' While Bolton fans were praised for keeping their humour despite relegation, the '*brash new stand*' at Craven Cottage was criticised as being '*smug, expensive, empty*'.

The other significant phenomenon of the mid 1980s was the fanzine explosion. Based loosely on the format of the punk fanzines of 1976, these homespun football publications often took their names from the titles of alternative pop songs. England's *When Saturday Comes* was inspired by an Undertones album track while Scotland's *The Absolute Game* owed its name to a Skids single. Like the home-stapled punk pages which preceded them, these fanzines approached football with an abrasive, irreverent sensibility more akin to the style of the weekly rock press.

The fanzines, in tune with the burgeoning indie mentality in music, aired views that were not being voiced elsewhere. They became an arena for ideological warfare, spoke out against racism on the terraces and criticised a complacent football establishment. For a few years – at least until their best writers were snapped up by the broadsheet newspapers and glossy monthly magazines – the fanzines gave football a sense of humour and a formidable conscience.

Prior to the purely football fanzines, two other style-slanted publications tapped into the links between music, youth culture and the terraces. A pair of emerging DJs, Terry Farley and Andy Weatherall, produced

Boys Own. And in Liverpool, Peter Hooton, also the singer with The Farm, edited *The End*, a genuine forerunner of the football fanzines.

'The idea of *The End* was to create a *Private Eye* for football supporters in Liverpool,' says Hooton. 'We wanted to attack every movement that was perceived as fashionable and we wanted to make people laugh. People used to say that we would never get football supporters to buy a fanzine, particularly one that also included music, and trying to sell the first few issues was almost impossible. But soon people realised what it was all about. It mentioned things which were relevant to their lives. It was aimed at fans who went to away matches. The supporters who went to away games in the 1980s were a unique group of people. Joe Strummer, the singer of The Clash, once described them as the vanguard of the working classes. I'm not so sure about that, but they were a distinct group who dressed in a unique way that set them aside.

'Before the World Cup in 1990, it was unfashionable to talk about football fans, about casuals or whatever you wanted to call them. Now the look that they pioneered has completely infiltrated the mainstream. The Oasis or Blur styles are basically a continuation of the way that football fans used to dress in the 1980s. The current styles provide a real link to the past. If you go to any sleepy English village now, you'll find young people wearing the sort of clothing that was the staple of any mid-1980s casual. Training shoes and expensive tracksuits have become the mainstream.'

As a football fan, editor of a streetwise style bible and emerging singer, Liverpool supporter Hooton was ideally placed to observe the collision between the cultures that characterised the era: 'Football was unfashionable in London media circles during the 1980s. It was looked down on as a horrific game. But it was never unfashionable in the circles I mixed in. And, if it was unhip elsewhere, a lot of football fans liked those anti-fashion aspects. It was as if football fans were public enemy number one and being a football fan was tantamount to being an anarchist. As a band, The Farm never particularly adopted football. But there was a certain casual image, so maybe we reflected it.

'The rehabilitation of football since 1990, however, has been the perfect media campaign. If Saatchi and Saatchi had orchestrated it, they would have won every advertising award going. Considering that people were worried about the very survival of football during the 1980s, the change has been dramatic. Between the mid-1980s and the 1990s, things have changed. Even the notion of Pavarotti providing the theme music for the World Cup would have been unthinkable in 1985.'

As a pop writer on *New Musical Express* in the 1980s, the underground links between music and football fuelled many of the features I wrote at the time. It seemed perfectly natural to be interviewing Pat Nevin, Chris Waddle or John Barnes one week and Paul Weller, The Housemartins or U2 the next. In meeting the more switched-on young players of the time, the growing mutual admiration between football and music also became apparent. While Nevin, with his sideswept fringe, heavy over-coat and Joy Division lapel badge, seemed to be the typical John Peel lis-tener, Charlie Nicholas appeared to model his entire look on U2's Bono Vox. 'My two heroes are Kenny Dalglish and Bono,' Nicholas told me. 'I remember the first time I heard 'I Will Follow' on the radio up in Glasgow. I just thought it was brilliant, so I went out and bought the *Boy* album the next day. Before I go to a match, I always play U2. It makes me want to go out onto the pitch and really have a go.'

If Nicholas and Nevin – plus fellow Scottish stars such as Brian McClair of Celtic and Manchester United and John Colquhoun of Hearts – were among the first players to contradict the straight, stereo-typed image of the professional footballer in the 1980s, others followed in their slipstream, with former punk Stuart Pearce of Nottingham Forest and the erudite Graeme Le Saux of Chelsea and Blackburn Rovers among the most prominent.

On the music front, meanwhile, the late 1980s witnessed the acid house movement. The 1988 summer of love and the rise of the so-called equity culture were at least partly responsible for a decline in football hooliganism. Reflecting the changing national mood, the official England song for the 1990 World Cup was an out-and-out dance track. The single was recorded by New Order, a group whose only previous connection with football had been in performing the theme music for the Granada television programme *Best And Marsh*. Written largely by the band's key-board player Gillian Gilbert, with lyrics by comedian Keith Allen and a rap by Liverpool's John Barnes, the track had originally been called 'E For England'. It was one of the most memorable pop records ever connected with football. Alongside Gazza's tears, Pavarotti's 'Nessun Dorma' and the 'no alla violenza' shirts popularised by, among others, The Farm, the song became stitched into the fabric of the football played during *Italia 90*.

'The FA came to us and made it clear that the song had to distance itself from hooliganism,' New Order singer Bernard Sumner told *NME* in 1990. 'Hence the *'love's got the world in motion'* line. It's an anti-hooligan song, but there's a deliberate ambiguity about the words in that they don't have to refer to football. Pop and football are nearer than they have been for a long time. From our point of view, there has been a football element to our fans for about six years. At the same time, there was no way I could have written a football song, which is why Keith Allen wrote them.'

With the 1990 World Cup also being commemorated by the Pop Will Eat Itself single 'Cicciolina', football entered the 1990s on the back of some of the most musically-credible songs ever released around the game, a trend that gathered pace with *Euro 96*. As well as 'Three Lions', the tournament was celebrated by songs such as 'Kickabout' by Teenage Fanclub, 'Beat My Goal' by Collapsed Lung and 'England's Irie' by Black Grape.

By the late 1990s, however, some dissenting voices were raised about the enduring crossover. Writing in *Vox*, music critic David Stubbs called for an end to the football-pop vortex. Arguing that 'indie sensibilities' had improved neither football or music, he claimed that things had reached a 'degenerate, laddish nadir'. While Stubbs had a point, the element of mediocrity that had crept into the mix of football and music was maybe just a consequence of yet another once-private party becoming part of the cultural mainstream. It appears that the two pastimes are destined to remain entwined for a while yet.

'My attitudes to football and music fluctuate all the time,' says singer and Chelsea fan Suggs. 'Sometimes I wish the two things were further apart, and I get fed up with hearing a New Order or Stone Roses track every time there is a football montage on television. Occasionally, I long for the era when you couldn't hear any music coming out of the Tannoy before kick-off at a big game. I remember a time when the match-day DJ at Stamford Bridge used to operate from a little box at the back of the North Stand. Cardiff City fans would spend the entire half-time interval throwing stones at him.

'Part of the charm of that bygone era was that football was anything but slick. Maybe that was what produced all the great football chants and songs. But there's no point in standing still. Time marches on and it looks as if we're all in it together these days.'

FROM A BATHTUB IN BURNAGE

IN BURNAGE

How football chants are created

Abathroom in Burnage, Greater Manchester, may well have been the scene for the creation of many a contemporary pop classic. The chances are that Noel Gallagher of Oasis, like all great songwriters, will have at some point found musical inspiration while singing or humming to himself in the bath. Gallagher certainly wrote many of the early Oasis hits while he was still based in the band's home-town. But memorable songs such as 'Live Forever', 'Cigarettes & Alcohol' and 'Shakermaker' weren't the only 1990s anthems likely to have roots in a Burnage bathtub. Some of the best new football chants of the 1990s – from 'Eric the King' to 'It's Poborsky' – also had their origins deep in the white enamel. Maybe it was something that they put in the water.

Pete Boyle, a twenty-seven-year-old office clerk and part-time DJ, is responsible for many of the songs that have boomed around Old Trafford over the past few seasons. A lifelong Manchester United sup-porter, he is an ardent cheerleader and chant creator. And some of his best songs in honour of the likes of Cantona, Cole, Giggs and Scholes have been composed in the bath. While many fans are dismayed by what they see as the decline in the level of chanting at British football in the 1990s, Boyle is one of the few individuals who are doing something about it. He talks about his role in the writing and introduction of new football songs with an almost evangelical zeal.

Boyle had some poems about Manchester United published when he was still at school. But his songwriting debut came at the start of the 1992-93 season. Encouraged by his success in writing farewell songs for departing colleagues at work, he applied the same procedure – adapting a traditional song or a pop hit with fresh lyrics – to the penning of songs of praise for his beloved football team.

The most obvious starting point was Eric Cantona, for whom Boyle reworked the 1968 Scaffold hit 'Lily The Pink'. The song's melody had been popular at Old Trafford once before, with United fans adopting it during the late Sixties to salute Denis Law. It had also been sung by Wolves fans at Molineux in honour of Derek Dougan and by Manchester City supporters drinking to Colin Bell. But it was one of those infectious uptempo tunes that had been dormant for the best part of two decades as far as football singing was concerned. The new United version eulogised Monsieur Cantona as "*Eric The King*", crowned in song as "*the leader of our football team*" and "*the greatest centre forward that the world has ever seen*". Boyle would often instigate the song himself at Old Trafford by standing up and waving his hands in the air during the chorus as he sang. In all, he wrote eight verses for his epic salute to the United striker, his efforts being rewarded when the song got voted most popular chant of the season in a club fanzine.

'I'd never claim to be a good singer,' explains Boyle. 'From an early age, though, I realised that I could write words and hold down a tune. Some people sit in the bath and think about the week ahead or the D-I-Y chores that they have to do. I just wallow there and write songs. I'm always calling my other half up the stairs and asking her for a pen and some paper because I've just had a song idea. At one stage, I wanted to be in a band. But I was never a good enough musician. If I had met someone with musical talent, maybe things might have been different. I feel like a Morrissey waiting for my Johnny Marr. But if someone gives me a topic and a tune, I can write a lyric for it.

'Where football chants are concerned, there are no golden rules. But a chant usually has to be short and sweet in order to catch on. It also helps if the melody comes from a well-known song. As far as getting a new song started, there are two stages. If you have a chant that you really want to get going, you must distribute the lyrics via a fanzine or in the pub before the game. After that, you've just got to have the nerve to stand up inside the ground and start singing. From the age of about fourteen or fifteen, for some reason, I've just had the balls to get up and sing. With the arrival of all-seater grounds, there are fewer people with the confidence to get up and do that. These days, even when some supporters are singing along with the songs, you get other people asking you to sit down. And we have also had club stewards intervening. I've had to put up with all that, but I've come through.'

Having established the 'live' credentials of his bathtub rhapsodies, Boyle then decided to preserve some of his best chants on tape. With some fellow fans and a drunken accordion player, he recorded thirty-five songs in a small local studio and dubbed them onto a cassette. The tape was then copied and circulated among friends and fans. Entitled *Songs from the Bathtub – United We Sing*, the project began as a joke, but Boyle has since moved on to volumes two and three of his cassette series. One of the tapes fell into the hands of Jim White, a *Guardian* journalist and author of the Manchester United book *Are You Watching Liverpool*. White penned a review, claiming that the songs were 'foul-mouthed, amateurishly produced and full of juvenile spleen'. In other words, he thought they were excellent.

'Some people say that I should cut the swearing out of the songs,' says Boyle. 'But that would destroy the point, because these songs – both the ones I write and the traditional United chants – are the songs that the fans actually sing. The problem with some of the glossier football CDs around is that the songs aren't the ones actually sung by fans. I'd never include anything racist or homophobic in a song and I'd never write or record anything with right-wing sentiments. But swearing is different. Whether people like it or not, swearing is part of the football fan's language.'

One of Boyle's homespun cassettes subsequently landed in the lap of United fan and independent label owner Jim Phelan. The result was a CD debut for the Burnage superfan, who contributed 'The Twelve Days of Cantona', 'The Grand Old King Eric' and, inevitably, 'Eric the King' to an album released in tribute to the Frenchman on Phelan's Exotica label in 1995. The CD reached number eleven in the independent chart and led to an early morning appearance for Boyle on Channel 4's *Big Breakfast*. As far as his recording career is concerned, however, Boyle has so far resisted any temptation to recruit a guest singer with greater technical ability.

'Getting a proper vocalist in to sing would be missing the point,' he argues. 'When I recorded 'Eric the King', it was a way of saying that ordinary football fans can go into a studio and sing an ordinary football song and get it on to a CD. If we got some cheesy girl singer to come in and re-record the song, it would be missing the point. I don't think any of the players have ever been offended by any of our songs. Eric Cantona was very proud and thanked me for doing the song when I met him while David May loved having a song dedicated to him.

'I did a song for Brian McClair based on the Elvis hit 'His Latest Flame'. The chorus saluted him – "*McClair's the name of United's flame*" – while the verses told the story of his career. He was wiping tears of laughter from his face when he heard it.' The Scottish striker, however, wasn't as flattered by another song which favourably compared his trophy-winning successes with those of a certain Newcastle-born centre forward who refused to sign for United: 'That song began "*Brian McClair, he may be fat, but he's got more medals than the greedy twat*". But, despite the references to his expanding waistline, Brian did acknowledge the song as he warmed up for a match.'

But just as Alan Shearer refused to put pen to paper for Alex Ferguson, so some of Pete Boyle's songs failed to gain a foothold among the Old Trafford faithful. Some remain as pub songs, either because the lyrics are too complex or the melodies too obscure to be adopted by a home crowd of over 50,000. One attempt to glorify Teddy Sheringham in song by adapting 'Sweet and Tender Hooligan' by The Smiths never made it out of the bar, although 'Neville Neville' – a chant which draws on David Bowie's 1974 single 'Rebel Rebel' – did surface briefly at White Hart Lane when Manchester United visited Spurs for the opening match of the 1997-98 season. There are also some United players whose names do not lend themselves to song as readily as others. Eric Cantona and Teddy Sheringham benefit hugely from their all-important three-syllable surnames while Andy Cole has the obvious advantage of a name which rhymes with 'goal'. But winger David Beckham, despite his superlative ability, is acclaimed in song with far less regularity than some of the other Old Trafford heroes.

One timeworn song popular in the city's pubs and clubs in the Fifties, 'The Manchester United Calypso', made a surprise reappearance at Old Trafford in the 1997-98 season. Originally recorded by Edric Connor, the song languished in obscurity until the early 1990s when it was revived via appearances on two separate compilation CDs of retro football songs, '*Bend It! 91*' and '*The Red Album*', both on the Exotica label. Apparently played over the Tannoy at Manchester Piccadilly station when United fans travelled down to London for the the 1957 FA Cup Final against Aston Villa, the song could be heard booming out of the J Stand at Old Trafford when the home side faced Holland's Feyenoord in the Champions League in October 1997, more than four decades later.

'You wouldn't have thought that a song like that would get going, but it has really become popular in the pubs and now inside the ground,' says Boyle, who is justifiably proud of Manchester United's singing heritage. 'The great songs of the 1960s and early 1970s are still sung now. Back then, lyric sheets were handed out on the Stretford End and the songs would take off in a massive way. I've got some video footage of crowds from the 1960s and you can hear the songs being sung by just about everyone in the stadium. People might have sung in little groups before then, but that was when the chants really seemed to take off.'

The adoption of the Oasis hit 'Wonderwall' by Manchester City fans in the 1995-96 season did not escape the attention of the United faithful. Boyle, mischievously, even maintains the song was sung at Old Trafford before it swept Maine Road, though this claim probably needs to be taken with a large pinch of bath salt. Once the track became so heavily associated with their municipal rivals, however, the United fans, in time-honoured fashion, devised an alternative version to sing back at City, as Boyle explains.

'Instead of finishing the song with "*after all, we've got Alan Ball*", as the City fans do, our variation finished on the pay-off line "*with Alan Ball, you're gonna win fuck all*". We also sing a version of "Don't Look Back In Anger" as "Don't Look Back In Envy". So many football chants are adapted from pop hits that Oasis are bound to feature. I even did one for City based on "Stand By Me" from *Be Here Now*. It was called 'Stand By Lee', advising the City fans to stand by Francis Lee who was the club's chairman at the time.'

United's phenomenal success since 1992 – and their reputation for attracting glory-hunting fans – has made them the most hated team in Britain. Anti-United feeling hit a new peak in November 1997 as choruses of '*stand up if you hate Man U*', an alternative national anthem of the late 1990s, echoed around Wembley throughout the friendly between England and Cameroon. The England team that night contained four United players, with midfielder Paul Scholes scoring one of the goals.

'United are hated in a way that even Liverpool, when they were at their peak in the 1980s, were not,' says Boyle. 'But that's not unique. The top teams in every country across Europe – Juventus in Italy, Bayern in

Germany and Rosenberg in Norway – appear to be hated by the rest of the fans in their home country. When Manchester United play in Europe now, the fans don't sing *"are you watching Liverpool"* or *"are you watching Newcastle"* anymore. They sing *"are you watching England"* in response to the England fans singing anti-United songs at Wembley. The hatred for Manchester United among England supporters is ridiculous. A large proportion of England squad for the 1998 World Cup and, potentially, half of the team for the European Championships in the year 2000 were groomed at Old Trafford.'

The practice of football chants being distributed on lyric sheets and in fanzines is a common one. It is also one that is not confined just to British fans. When Aston Villa played Helsingborg of Sweden in the First Round of the UEFA Cup in September 1996, supporters arriving in Scandinavia from Birmingham were met by a local man wielding a printed songsheet of all the club's chants. The fan, a Villa follower, had taped episodes of *Match Of The Day* and transcribed the songs from his VHS cassettes.

It is in the pubs before and after matches, however, that many of the most memorable songs first appear, often doing the rounds for months and even years before finally making it into football grounds. With many of the old, indigenous urban taverns now replaced by European-style bars, particularly in the home counties, the tradition of the pub singalong is not as powerful in the 1990s as it was in previous decades. But, in northern strongholds such as Manchester, Liverpool, Newcastle and Glasgow, local pubs still provide a fertile breeding ground for football songs.

'There are lots of Liverpool songs that are only ever really sung in pubs,' says Peter Hooton, ex-singer with The Farm. 'If you go into some of the pubs around Anfield on a Saturday night, you'll witness something akin to a Eurovision Song Contest of football chants. Many of the chants don't even make it into the stadium. But most of them that do start in the pubs. In the 1970s, the songs began much more spontaneously inside the ground. When people were standing up on a crowded terrace, the good songs tended to spread quite quickly.

'There are still pockets in the ground where fans sing in much the same way as they did then. I know of one guy who has a committee to decide what songs can and cannot be sung. He will often veto a song if it has already been sung by another club. Generally, however, people are much more self-conscious now that they are sitting down.'

BRASS
IN POCKET

Graham Pell usually hooks up with Paul, Dave, Maggie, Keith, John and Stewart at about midday in an Irish bar in the centre of Barnsley. For away games, the troupe tend to rendezvous much earlier and stop for a few beers once they are *en route* in a hired minibus. For Saturday home matches, though, noon is perfect. The instruments come out almost immediately and the music starts just as the first rounds arrive. Graham himself plays trumpet, as does Maggie. Additional brass comes from trombonists Stewart and John with the rest of the crew contributing drumming and percussion.

The seven-strong ensemble usually play for about an hour outside the bar, helping to attract the lunchtime drinkers. At about one o'clock, they parade slowly through the town centre playing football songs, picking up supporters as they go, before decamping to another pub closer to the football ground. There they play a selection of Barnsley-related songs for another half-an-hour. When the weather is fine, they set up in the car park outside, their red scarves, replica tops and club sweatshirts lending a heavy crimson hue to South Yorkshire's urban landscape. Eventually, at about 2.30 pm, they march up Grove Street to Oakwell.

About a hundred yards from the stadium, they always stop and play a song outside the same telephone box, religiously serenading the caller inside. The stop-off has become such an established pre-match ritual that a gaggle of red-scarfed Barnsley supporters are invariably waiting for them outside the kiosk. By the time they reach the ground, like an itinerant group of footballing Pied Pipers, they have always picked up a strong contingent of admirers.

Inside Oakwell, the small troupe set out their stall in the Ora Stand and strike up their match-day anthem in its full splendour. To the tune of 'Blue Moon' – the old Elvis Presley ballad that has for years been a signature tune for fans of both Manchester City and Crewe Alexandra – they salute their team. The Oakwell faithful immediately respond in song. Instead of the usual lyrics, however, the Barnsley fans use the song to compare their heroes to a team of South American legends. And so the chant goes up: '*Brazil – it's just like watching Brazil, it's just like watching Brazil, it's just like watching Brazil.*'

Barnsley's version of 'Blue Moon' started during the 1996-97 season, when the club won promotion to the Premiership by playing football so neat that one Ora Stand regular deemed it worthy of the Brazilians. It was from this chant that Graham and his cohorts – known as the Ora Stand Band – gained a reputation as a samba group. Their style, however, isn't as relentless as that of the Latin horn players and drummers who accompany South American sides to World Cups. The Ora Stand Band take the odd breather between songs, particularly during matches.

In addition to 'Blue Moon', they play a medley of well-loved football songs. They also play 'Walking in a Wilson Wonderland' for manager Danny Wilson and at least one song in honour of former Oakwell folk hero Ronnie Glavin, a Scot who later became the manager of local Unibond League side Emley, whom he took to the third round of the FA Cup in January 1998. Corinthians at heart, the band then attempt to play a song associated with the opposing team. When West Ham opened the 1997-98 season at Oakwell, the band played 'Bubbles'. A week later, they entertained Chelsea with 'Blue is the Colour'. And, in December, serenaded the Toon Army with 'Blaydon Races'.

At the final whistle, the band retire to one of the pubs visited earlier. Depending largely on how the match went, their trek back to the bar is accompanied either by 'Blue Moon' or a sombre death march. They will usually play on for about an hour, generally dispersing at around six o'clock.

They made their Oakwell debut in April 1997 at the final match of

Barnsley's promotion season. Club representatives had asked them to perform in order to encourage the capacity 18,000 crowd to sing, thus enhancing the team's chances of beating Yorkshire rivals Bradford City and gaining the three points needed to ensure Premiership football. As musicians, the group members had previously met through the Barnsley Music Centre and were long-term friends. Some had been playing for twenty years in local bands and all were regulars at Oakwell. For the Bradford match – which was won 2-0 by Barnsley with goals from Paul Wilkinson and Clint Marcelle – the band were a compact quintet. By the start of the Premiership season in August 1997, the ranks had swollen to seven, with a fourth drummer occasionally making the group a noisy eight-piece.

'Football is a real passion in Barnsley,' says thirty-four-year-old Pell, who works for a company which manufactures playground equipment in Barnsley. 'You can tell that by the away support that the club enjoys. Even when it isn't doing so well, the team still gets very loyal and vocal support. So the band just feeds off the enthusiasm of the other Barnsley fans.'

While South Yorkshire has a proud tradition of producing colliery bands, the Ora Stand group align themselves more with the Hillsborough Kop Band at nearby Sheffield Wednesday. The Wednesday brass was itself influenced by the two separate bands which regularly accompany the Dutch national side. But the two Yorkshire groups are also maintaining a tradition that has seen percussion at Sheffield United, a band consisting of drummers and a trumpeter at Preston North End and a famous bugle player by the deed-poll-changed name of John Portsmouth Football Club Westwood at Fratton Park.

'We have a lot in common with the Wednesday band,' says Pell. 'One of the guys who runs the Wednesday group helped to get us going. But we would claim that the difference between the two outfits is firstly that we can actually play our instruments while they can't. The other thing is that they tend to perform continuously through the game, usually playing the same song, which must get on people's nerves. We prefer to play in short bursts. Our claims usually cause a fair bit of banter between the two clubs.'

The group take their instruments to away games after first checking with the opposing club whether it is okay for them to play. They have been refused access to Pride Park by Derby County and to Selhurst Park by both Wimbledon and Crystal Palace. But most of the big Premiership clubs – including Manchester United, Liverpool and Everton – have let them play.

'The opposing fans have always been brilliant,' says Pell. 'We have an affinity with the fans of most other clubs. I hope that's not just because they feel sorry for us, because we did suffer some pretty heavy defeats away from home in the Premiership. After we had visited Old Trafford, the United fans asked us to play outside the stadium after the match. We were then invited to play a concert in the British Legion Club in Manchester.'

Reactions in their home town, however, have occasionally been slightly less favourable: 'We have had a few negative comments from folk in Barnsley. With Sheffield being so close, a lot of people think we've just copied the Wednesday band. But that's not the case. It really rubs the rag with us when people say we're Owls fans and not Barnsley supporters, because we've all been regulars at Oakwell for years. Our families and friends, however, have always backed us to the hilt. With all the euphoria surrounding the run-in to promotion from Division One in the spring of 1997, family life often took second place to the band. It sounds terrible to say such a thing, but that was how it was for a lot of people in the town. But, having said that, all the family came along to the match against Bradford City. Clinching promotion turned out to be a real family occasion.'

Winning a place in the Premiership for the first time was also an excuse for the noisiest and street celebrations the town had ever seen: 'That Saturday night in Barnsley was something that will never be relived unless the team win the FA Cup. It had been a really hot day, so we all went back into the centre of town and opened the sun roof on the car. In Wellington Street, where there are a lot of pubs next door to one another, we came down the street leading a convoy of cars all bearing flags.

'It was just like being in Spain or Italy when one of their big clubs celebrates winning the championship. When we got to the end of the road, the police asked us to stop. We thought they were going to turn us round. Instead they started their car sirens and just told all the fans to stick together. The Bradford City supporters had been great too. It was a big game for them, because they were struggling for points at the other end of the table. But their supporters stopped and cheered at the end of the game as the Barnsley team celebrated promotion. In return, a lot of Barnsley fans went over to the Pulse Stadium at Valley Parade to see Bradford win their following match, which helped them to avoid relegation.'

Like the Brazilian musicians before them and the groups which have serenaded African nations such as Cameroon and Nigeria in World Cups, the Barnsley band have become an essential part of most of the games involving their team. The only cautionary note should be the one sounded by a Dutchman at the end of his country's *Euro 96* campaign. Holland's progress through the tournament had been accompanied by the two brass sections which follow them everywhere. After losing on penalties to the French in their quarter-final at Anfield, however, one supporter was in no mood for music. 'Now,' he demanded at the end of the match, angrily clenching his fists. 'Where's that bloody trombone player ...'

PARKLIFE

The Double-winning Tottenham Hotspur captain Danny Blanchflower famously described the noise of a football crowd as the oxygen that the players breathed. But, from a footballer's point of view, that air isn't always as fresh as a Swiss Alpine morning. If a player's confidence is low and a football crowd start chanting abuse at him, the fumes inhaled are sometimes very stale indeed. When he was playing for Everton in the 1980s, the Scottish winger Pat Nevin remembers hearing one of his own team's supporters singing a song of vilification about him. 'It was,' recalls Nevin, 'like a stab in the heart.'

Footballers are affected in different ways by abuse and praise from supporters. In 1996, the Nottingham Forest forward Jason Lee was constantly subjected to the refrain '*he's got a pineapple on his head*', a reference to his distinctive funki-dred hairstyle. The chant cropped up with such monotonous regularity on Frank Skinner and David Baddiel's *Fantasy Football League*, however, that Forest eventually transfer-listed the young striker, alleging that his career had been adversely affected by his ongoing televised torment.

In 1997, Manchester United's David Beckham reacted angrily when West Ham United fans taunted him at Old Trafford with obscene chants concerning his relationship with Victoria Adams of the Spice Girls. After

Roy Keane had scored one of the goals in a 2-1 win for United, Beckham turned to confront his tormentors with an aggressive flourish. Four months later, when Beckham was subjected to similar abuse during an FA Cup third-round tie at Chelsea, the young international again react-ed to the insults, although this time his response was more measured: he merely cupped a hand to his ear as if to enquire why the chants had dried up as he celebrated his second goal of the game.

Most professional footballers and officials have acquired a thick cloak of mental toughness to help them to deal with personal insults. But the effect that the chants and insults *can* have, particularly on those with families, is still often overlooked. Former referee Neil Midgley – a man who once joked that he only took up the job once his eyesight started to fail – recalls being aware of the fact that his wife was in the stadium during a First Division game. 'At one stage, a whole row of sup-porters stood up in the area where she was seated and started giving me the V-sign,' he says. 'When I asked her later what she did, she replied that she didn't want them to know who she was so she started doing it too!'

Such anecdotes are amusing, but there are serious matters underlying them. While vocal support can make a huge difference to a team, and a passionate crowd can be worth a one- or two-goal start to the home side, there is an obvious downside for the men on the park. If the taunts turn nasty, players need to summon up a form of sporting psychology to deal with the brain-rattling insults and cheerfully-chanted invective.

For most players, though, hearing their name chanted in unison for the very first time is a special moment, as Pat Nevin explains: 'I remem-ber the first time fans sang my name. I was a part-timer with the Glasgow club Clyde in Scottish Division Two. The ground, Shawfield, had a dog track and was sparsely populated, so the crowd noise didn't have a big effect. But it was still nice. It was also great when Scotland fans sang my name, particularly as I was never a regular international-ist. But the first time the singing really struck me was after I went to Chelsea in 1983.

'At Stamford Bridge, the chanting of the fans was brilliant. It was always a complete confidence booster. Even when things weren't going so well, the Chelsea fans never once wavered in their encouragement. At some clubs, players tend to get a honeymoon period when the fans get behind them. At Chelsea, for me at least, that never ended. The sup-porters took to me early on and never got on my back.

'There were a few games when I would be having a stinker. Playing on the wing, I would be unable to get past the opposing full-back. Because the fans could see that I was really trying, however, they kept chanting my name. And that always had a profound effect. Instead of playing the easy pass – playing the percentages, as they say in football – the singing would give me the confidence to continue taking on that full-back. At the end of the game, I might have got past him twice in twenty attempts. But that would sometimes be enough for me to set up two goals and give us something from the game. In those instances, the chanting of the fans was what made been the difference. There were undoubtedly occasions where their songs won us the game.

'The Chelsea fans were inspiring to play in front of. When the team went through tough times, the fans always gave them a lift, particularly away from home. Having watched a lot of football in London, I came to realise that each of the big clubs – Chelsea, Arsenal, Spurs and West Ham – had its own fan culture. For a London player, the best supporters to play for were Chelsea fans. If that sounds biased, it isn't meant to be.

'I sometimes went to see Spurs play midweek matches in Europe in the early 1980s. I wanted to learn by watching Glenn Hoddle, Ossie Ardiles and Mike Hazard in action at close quarters. So, rather than sit in the stand, I stood on the terraces. The thing that most amazed me was how different the supporters were from Chelsea fans. The feeling, the degree of encouragement, just wasn't the same. Why that should be, I just don't know. There is no big religious or geographical divide, as there is in other cities, and the fans of all the London clubs basically come from the same background. But the Chelsea fans follow their team with a passion that was closer to the sort of support that Celtic have in Glasgow.'

For all the passion they provided, there was a racist element in the Chelsea crowd of the 1980s which didn't appeal to Nevin. Opposed to bigotry of any kind, the nimble winger found himself in conflict with some of his own fans over the issue of racism in football. These differences reached a head after a section of the Chelsea support barracked one of their own players, the black striker Paul Cannoville, in an away match against Crystal Palace at Selhurst Park. Nevin, having scored Chelsea's winning goal, used the platform afforded him by the post-match press conference and radio interviews to condemn the actions of the boo-boys.

'Instead of talking about the game,' says Nevin. 'I just told the jour-
nalists that I was disgusted with the Chelsea fans for the way in which
they were treating one of our players. Before the next game, David
Speedie, Kerry Dixon and myself all walked out on to the pitch alongside Cannoville in a show of support. Normally, the fans would always
sing my name, or the names of Speedie and Dixon, first. But this time
they started singing Paul's name first. It was one of the most moving
moments of my football career. A group of players had said something
and it had had an effect on the fans. It wasn't just my comments. It was
also the actions of David and Kerry, in showing solidarity, that helped
to turn the tables on racist chanting. I'm not saying that we eliminated
it. But it was a lovely moment and it helped to point the way forward.
It was an important turning point. It gave the whole team, not just the
black players, a genuine lift.'

Nevin maintains that players are able to rise above abusive chanting the
majority of the time. Occasionally, however, a football song manages to
hit a nerve and a footballer snaps mentally: 'If a crowd get to a player at
the right time – the wrong time, as it were – they will certainly affect
him. If a player's confidence is low, or if there are things happening in
his private life, then the fans can destroy him. Eric Cantona was widely
criticised over the Selhurst Park episode, when he jumped into the
crowd, but that criticism doesn't take account of the extreme racist
abuse that he was subjected to. Like most players, he could ignore the
general chanting. But he was pushed over the edge by one specific taunt.
I know plenty of people within football who still view his actions in a
positive light.

'Most players have personalities that help them to overcome or
ignore negative chanting. Those players who aren't thick-skinned
enough to withstand the terrace taunts tend not to make it to the top.
They tend to drop out of football at an earlier stage. They don't have the
strength of character necessary to be a professional. Some clubs even try
to weed out the weaker personalities at youth level by adopting regimes
that test mental toughness. The clubs employ coaches who verbally
abuse young players, giving them a hard time just to see whether they
can stand up to the pressure.

'Some clubs adopt a system that is more like an army regime. The
coach will try and break a young player to test whether he is up to the

emotional and mental rigours of the professional game. It isn't because they hate the player. It's a case of identifying weak points and working out whether a player can handle it. It happened to me when I was sixteen. One particular coach put me through hell. Then, after my final year as a youth player, he took me aside and explained that there had been nothing personal in it. He had just wanted to make me aware of what I would have to deal with. The fact that I came through that has meant that even the most abusive terrace chants have never had an adverse effect on me.

'There is no point in wrapping your youth team players up in cotton wool for five years. A young player needs preparation for the day on which he walks out on to a football pitch and is called every name under the sun. If you haven't had the right kind of character building, you will simply not be able to handle the sound of 40,000 people singing something insulting about you. And it's not just the players who are affected. Most players will have their wives, girlfriends or parents watching from the stand and that knowledge can affect a player. Professionals themselves are usually thick-skinned enough to laugh off terrace taunts. But sometimes they will react simply because they are concerned about the feelings of their own family members in the stand.

'You expect abuse from opposition fans and you can often use that to your advantage. It can make you angry or more determined to do well. If the opposing team's supporters have singled you out for an nasty chant, it shows that they are worried about you. It sounds perverse, but a player can actually have his confidence boosted by having the opposition fans singing offensive things about him,' says Nevin.

The American international goalkeeper Kasey Keller, who has played top-level football in England for both Millwall and Leicester City, studied sociology to degree level at Portland University in Oregon. One of his specialist subjects involved a study of the fan sub-cultures in football. Having played football in both the US and England, he is well placed to compare the nature of soccer supporters – and the noise they generate – in the two countries.

'The fans in America don't sing nearly as much as they do in England,' says Keller. 'There is one group of dedicated fans, called Uncle Sam's Army, who support the national team abroad in tournaments like the World Cup or the Copa America. Those guys are trying hard to change the culture and start more singing at games in the States. American fans are accustomed to sports like basketball, baseball and grid-iron football where there are very distinct times to cheer.

'American fans are used to sitting in virtual silence for a large part of a major sports event. They are conditioned to sit and absorb the action until something specific happens and elicits a loud cheer. So, in soccer, they obviously cheer when their team scores a goal. But they don't quite know how to support their team vocally during the rest of the game. Many American fans are still unfamiliar with the intricacies of football.

'Even though most of them are now well educated as to the written rules of the game, they don't always understand what represents good play and what represents poor play. Generally, they don't yet appreciate a great pass, a good saving tackle or the imaginative movement of players off the ball. But good football doesn't necessarily have to mean lots of goals and British fans appreciate that more than their American counterparts.

'The other thing, as far as singing is concerned, is that a lot of chants are brought about by the tension between two groups of supporters. In America, you don't get anything like the same degree of away support, because the distances are much greater. You won't get many fans of Washington DC United travelling to watch their team play a league match away to San Jose Clash on the other side of the country. Because of that, you just don't get the same sort of banter between the fans.'

Before moving to Millwall in 1991, Keller had only watched English football on television. He admits to being struck by the sheer volume of noise generated by the crowds at the Den when he first came to London. As a goalkeeper, Keller's proximity to the crowd make him a prime target for abusive fans, a problem he shares with a touchline-hugging winger like Nevin. The two most common taunts aimed at goalkeepers in the 1990s are the ubiquitous cry of '*you're shit – aah!*' that accompanies every goal-kick, and the more recent '*dodgy keeper, dodgy keeper*' chant. Keller feels, however, that the content of the singing hasn't developed or progressed in any significant way in the time he has been in Britain.

'For the most part, I seem to hear the same chants as when I first came over, and I'm sure a lot of them have been the same for decades. Chants are always going to be directed at keepers. But very few of them are particularly creative or even that malicious. One of the most enjoyable things about at Millwall fans was that the singing was at least pretty witty and original. You could always have a laugh about it. The Millwall fans were superb when they were behind you and I was lucky in that I had a good rapport with them. Other players who have played for the club mightn't agree with that, because they can also be pretty nasty if they are against you.

'The Leicester City supporters tend to chant "*U-S-A! U-S-A!*" when I pull off a good save. There's one incident I remember in particular. It was during the replay of the Coca-Cola Cup final against Middlesbrough at Hillsborough in 1997. Steve Claridge had just scored what turned out to be the winning goal for Leicester and I was immediately called on to make an important one-on-one save against Middlesbrough's Brazilian midfield player Emerson. It was amazing to hear the fans chanting "*U-S-A! U-S-A!*" at that moment.'

PASS, SHOOT. GOAL!

One of the earliest known recordings of a football song dates from 1927, when the pre-match singing of the Cup Final hymn 'Abide With Me' was captured for posterity on the relatively primitive audio equipment of the late Twenties. The match – in which Cardiff City beat Arsenal 1-0 at Wembley – was doubly significant in that it was also the only time the Cup was won by a team from outside England. As well as 'Abide With Me', the sputtering, crackling recording made in May 1927 featured the sound of the same 92,000 distant, eerie Wembley voices singing the traditional Welsh anthem 'Land Of My Fathers'.

In the seventy-plus years that have elapsed since that day, the football record has entertained, provoked and irritated successive generations. From the traditional memento of a cheerily inane Cup Final single, the art of the football single has progressed to encompass a deluge of novelty hits, earnest musical whirls from senior professionals who should have known better and numerous other sonic atrocities.

Yet the football record has survived and thrived. Its often kitsch appeal has regularly injected colour and character, plus heart and humour, into a game that sometimes takes itself far too seriously. And, every now and then, football has even produced the odd single of genuine musical merit or lyrical poignancy. The way in which the football record has altered in the seven decades since the Twenties has also paralleled the changing face of popular music since then: thus the simple, touching songs of the Thirties and Forties were gradually superseded by the calypsos of the Fifties, the pop tunes of the Sixties, the stomping Eurovision styles of the Seventies, the raps of the Eighties and the eclecticism of the Nineties.

The Thirties, following the momentous 1927 Cup Final recording, saw a spate of memorable football records. In 1931, Rochdale's Gracie Fields sang the jaunty, saucy 'Pass, Shoot, Goal', in which *the poor referee was kicked by three or four… right between the whistle and the half-time score.*" Our Gracie's effort was followed by 'Sandy The Goalkeeper' by Sandy Powell and the George Formby-esque 'I Do Like To See A Game Of Football' by Sidney Kyte & His Orchestra in 1932. The same year also witnessed a spoken-word disc to celebrate the FA Cup Final in which Newcastle United defeated Arsenal courtesy of a hotly-disputed goal.

The Forties were largely unproductive due to the aftermath of the Second World War. But a new vitality and creativity became apparent in the Fifties. The new sparkle was particularly conspicuous in a crop of superb football calypsos in the early part of the decade. One of the first manifestations of the enormous impact that immigrants from the Caribbean were to have on British popular culture, these songs – which were particularly popular in Manchester – saluted individual star players, favourite teams and even the game itself.

While Edric Connor's 'Manchester United Calypso' celebrated the Busby Babes, the city's twin successes of 1956 – when United won the League Championship and City landed the FA Cup – were acclaimed in striking style by the Lord Kitchener Fitzroy Coleman Band on 'The Manchester Football Double'. Later efforts, such as the 'Ipswich Football Calypso' of 1962 and the 'Leeds United Calypso' of 1964 had a slightly less authentic flavour but remain valid musical documents of the era. The tragic loss of eight members of Matt Busby's young United team in the Munich Air Disaster of 1958 was also commemorated in a moving song entitled 'The Flowers Of Manchester', a record that featured the side's Northern Irish goalkeeper Harry Gregg, a survivor of the fatal crash.

The Sixties began with Tottenham Hotspur in the ascendency. The North Londoners won the League and FA Cup double in 1961, the FA Cup again in 1962 and the European Cup-Winners' Cup in 1963, thus fully deserving the 'Tip Top Tottenham Hotspur' tag conveyed on them by The Totnamites, a vocal outfit in the easy-listening style of the Swingle Singers. On the dinner-jacketed front, England captain Billy Wright made 'The Sunshine Of Your Smile' while Welsh international John Charles, the 'Gentle Giant' who became a star of *Serie A* with Juventus, recorded two Italian-influenced epics in 'Love In Portofino' and 'La Fine'.

With the first links between football and pop music increasingly evident, the 1966 World Cup in England was accompanied by a plethora of vinyl, the most notable effort being 'World Cup Willie' by skiffle legend Lonnie Donegan. The most forgettable was the musically pompous 'Up There England', the first official single by a squad of England players. Club records were also on the increase. In Scotland, Rangers made 'Every Other Saturday' with assistance from comedian Lex McLean and their city rivals recorded the accordion-led 'Celtic, Celtic', both records dating from 1964. In England, meanwhile, the Old Trafford squad cut 'United United' while a group of Tottenham players, including Terry Venables and Joe Kinnear, released *The Spurs Go Marching On*, an EP containing pub favourites such as 'Bye Bye Blackbird' and 'When Irish Eyes Are Smiling'. From the same era, Jackie Charlton's 'Geordie Sunday' was a spoken-word epic worthy of Lee 'Wandrin' Star' Marvin.

The first football record to top the singles chart in Britain arrived when the England World Cup Squad of 1970 released 'Back Home' on the back of a wave of national optimism. The record's strident tone set the style for the club songs of the early Seventies such as Tottenham's 'Nice One Cyril' and Chelsea's 'Blue Is The Colour'. Other hits from the same era, most of them characterised by prominent bass and booming drums, included 'Good Old Arsenal', 'Leeds United', 'Sunderland All The Way', 'Viva El Fulham', West Ham's 'I'm Forever Blowing Bubbles' and a version of the Rubettes hit 'We Can Do It' by the 1976 Liverpool squad.

As well as the club singalongs, there were some best-forgotten solo efforts in the late Seventies and early Eighties. Kevin Keegan released two singles, 'England' and 'Head Over Heels In Love', while Nottingham Forest striker Justin Fashanu gatecrashed the early Eighties Britfunk party with 'Do It 'Cos You Like It'. The stars of European soccer got in on the act too, with legends such as Johan Cruyff, Giorgio Chinaglia and Franz Beckenbauer all making records. But – with the exception of Chas & Dave and their Spurs links – the old-style singalongs faded during the

Eighties and some players turned their attention to making records that strived, with varying degrees of success, for greater musical credibility.

The Tottenham and England pair of Glenn Hoddle and Chris Waddle had a hit in 1987 with 'Diamond Lights', a passable Eighties synthesiser pop single that was far less offensive than the dodgy haircuts the duo sported when they made an unlikely *Top Of The Pops* appearance. 'We're not saying that "Diamond Lights" is the greatest record ever made,' Hoddle said in an *NME* interview in 1987. 'But it's something we can be proud of.' A decade later, music fanatic Waddle stood defiantly by his recording debut. 'Even now, people still come up to me after games and talk about the single,' he told me in 1997. 'Glenn and I wanted to make a proper single instead of doing a song like "Nice One Cyril". So we did "Diamond Lights", it reached the top ten and we both enjoyed it. People might take the mickey out of it, but I didn't want to look back years later and think that I had the chance to make a record and didn't take it.'

Another progression came with 'Anfield Rap', Liverpool's 1988 FA Cup Final single. The record was the brainchild of the club's Australian midfielder Craig Johnston, who wrote the lyrics and even negotiated the deal which gave the single its release through Virgin Records. Produced by London dance music pioneer Derek B, the record was a watershed in its adoption of contemporary urban rhythms. In featuring the rapping of winger John Barnes, it also paved the way for the England hit 'World In Motion' by New Order two years later.

'I hate football records and I always have,' Johnston informed me in 1988. 'So I wanted to do something different with "Anfield Rap". I wanted to do something that was more contemporary. Wherever you go now, you hear club music. The house sound of Chicago and rap music are the dominant rhythms, so that was what we wanted. Rap records often have a DJ or MC taking the piss out of each other. The "Anfield Rap" is the members of a football team taking the piss out of one another. People are always asking about the Liverpool secret. Football managers come to Anfield from all over the world to try and work out what it is that makes us tick. I think this record captures some of the essence of the club.'

'It was a great record for the team to do,' added Barnes. 'Having been born in Jamaica, the first music I got into was reggae, but I am also into rap and soul. So I enjoyed doing "Anfield Rap". Rap crews are like football teams. If you look at Grandmaster Flash & The Furious Five, they are a genuine team, just like Liverpool.'

With 'World In Motion' dragging the football record further out of the Eurovision-style slumber of the late Seventies and early Eighties, the tone of football records became far more eclectic in the Nineties, a trend which culminated in 'Three Lions'. With Frank Skinner, David Baddiel and the Lightning Seeds having set a new benchmark, the Chelsea single for the 1997 FA Cup Final against Middlesbrough was another authentic fans' theme. Entitled 'Blue Day', it was sung by former Madness vocalist Suggs and featured an affectionate set of lyrics that, in the style of 'Three Lions', avoided the premature triumphalism that was such a cornerstone of the old-style football records.

'From my perspective, it was a good song because it was written from a fan's perspective,' says Suggs. 'Members of the Chelsea team joined in with some singing, but it was essentially a fan's song. Doing a football record was a challenge. It was something that I could never have done ten years earlier. But I was really excited that Chelsea were at Wembley and "Three Lions" had changed the perception of what was possible on a football song. It showed that a football single could be something for the fans rather than just a cash-in. I wanted "Blue Day" to combine the magic of the old chants with a more sensitive modern outlook.

'On the day of the match, supporters were singing the song on Olympic Way. That meant a lot to me. Then it was played just before kick-off and after the final whistle. They actually played it three times after the match, alternating it with "Blue Is The Colour". The Middlesbrough fans had long gone and there were only Chelsea fans in the stadium. By the third time it was played, all the Chelsea fans left were singing it. It was probably one of the best moments of my life. That might sound like an egotistical thing, but it was something more than that. It was really moving for me to hear the song being sung by so many old Chelsea die-hards and stalwarts who had suffered over the years. It was a fantastic feeling. If we had lost, of course, I would have felt cursed by the record for the rest of my life.'

Chelsea's noble Seventies anthem, 'Blue Is The Colour', was one of the old-fashioned football records that somehow managed to transcend its club. The fact that it was only usurped on Stamford Bridge match-days by 'Blue Day' in the 1997-98 season was indicative of one of the unique facets of football records: the age of a club's main anthem is an excellent indication of the period of time since the team last reached a final or won something. The more recent the anthem, the more successful the club.

'They now play "Blue Day" as the team come out,' says Suggs. 'Until recently, they used to play "Blue Is The Colour". To be honest, my personal preference is still for "Blue Is The Colour", which was a song that reminded me of the glory and style associated with Chelsea when I first started going to watch them. For me, "Blue Is The Colour" will always shine, in the same way that the team of the Seventies will always shine. I associate the song with an era when I was at my most impressionable, so it will always live with me.

'When I hear "Blue Is The Colour", I don't hear a bunch of blokes who couldn't sing trying to make a pop record. I see Peter Osgood in full cry or David Webb scoring the winner against Leeds in the 1970 FA Cup Final. I don't feel quite the same about my song, not yet anyway. Maybe I am too involved. Maybe there are younger Chelsea fans who feel the same about "Blue Day" as I did about "Blue Is The Colour". Maybe they will always associate that song with Chelsea winning the FA Cup in 1997. Dennis Wise told me that the Chelsea players were all desperate to win the Cup in 1997 to erase the memory of the Seventies team. In winning the FA Cup, they partly did that. It seems strange to say it, but that win has also meant that "Blue Day" partly erased the memory of "Blue Is The Colour".'

Chelsea have not been alone in linking up with a credible Nineties pop artist to make music. The Arsenal striker Ian Wright collaborated with Chris Lowe of The Pet Shop Boys on a one-off dance single and the FA Cup winning Chelsea manager Ruud Gullit had a hit single in his native Holland with 'Not The Dancing Kind'. Gullit has also played with a roots group called Reggae Revolution. Alexei Lalas, the goatie-bearded USA centre-back who had a spell with Padova in the Italian League, went one better in releasing an album of his own songs, *Far From Close*, on the eve of the 1994 World Cup. And two young British players – former QPR striker Daniele Dichio and Nottingham Forest's Paul McGregor – have also made a musical mark. Dichio toured the dance music hotspots of Ibiza, Tenerife and Magaluf under his DJ alias of Melo D while McGregor received some serious attention from the credible weekly music papers while fronting his guitar band Merc in 1996.

*　　　*　　　*

In addition to the occasional team song or solo offering with some musical merit, the early Nineties also saw the inexorable rise of the retro football album. Often superbly-packaged, these CDs have tapped into the burgeoning market for football memorabilia. The phenomena began in the
late Eighties when London-based independent record companies such as
él and Confection released their first football LPs. The business has since
blossomed through the activities of the Exotica and Cherry Red labels.

Exotica initially made an impression through the *Bend It!* series, a
string of four compilations, and have since released a batch of
Manchester United tributes, *Cantona, Georgie* and *The Red Album*. The
Bend It! CDs featured an outlandish mixture of archive material plus
new songs by obscure contemporary acts. Among the most notable
tracks in the latter category were 'Roger Milla Is My Number Nine
Dream' and 'Ryan Giggs We Love You' by the Rainbow Choir and 'Ooh
Gary Gary' by Her, the latter a tribute to Gary Lineker. Kitsch bub-
blegum pop numbers they may have been, but many of the *Bend It!*
songs picked up prime-time radio exposure in the early Nineties.

Cherry Red Records, meanwhile, embarked on an even more ambi-
tious programme of football albums in the mid Nineties. By the start of
1998, the London label had released 23 club-orientated song collec-
tions, from Aberdeen to Wimbledon, and were looking to expand their
catalogue at a rate of about ten new CDs every season.

The albums were painstakingly researched and compiled by Arsenal
fan and former music business talent broker Tim Madgwick. They sold
through club shops, magazines, local record shops and fanzines. Sales
generally numbered between four to five thousand per album, although
the Liverpool collection 'You'll Never Walk Alone' has sold a lot more,
courtesy of the club's huge supporters associations in Scandinavia.

'The football record has been around for far longer than the football
chant,' says Madgwick. 'You would have thought it was going to be the
other way around, but the singing at matches only really took off in tan-
dem with violence and hooliganism during the Sixties. As for the
albums, they are the perfect thing for the car on the journey to away
matches. The songs are not something you can take too seriously, but
the more we get into it, the more interesting it becomes.

'It might sound like something for anoraks and trainspotters, but
every club seems to have at least a couple of really good songs. The most
stunning thing is the variety. The West Ham one features a couple of

Adrian Sherwood tracks and the alternative comedian Sean Hughes did a track on the Palace one. Then there's "Tae The Dons From Donside" on the Aberdeen CD. That was by Cath & Jean, two female farmers from rural Aberdeenshire. They did the song as a laugh when Aberdeen won the European Cup-Winners' Cup in 1983. They couldn't believe that it had made it onto an album fifteen years later. A lot of football songs tend to live for a long time.'

PART TWO
THE SONGS

BY FAR THE
GREATEST TEAM

We're so good it's unbelievable,
We're so good it's unbelievable.

We are the champions,
(clap-clap-clap-clap-clap).

We're gonna win the league,
We're gonna win the league,
And now you're gonna believe us,
And now you're gonna believe us,
And now you're gonna believe us,
We're gonna win the league.

We shall not, we shall not be moved,
We shall not, we shall not be moved,
Just like a team that's gonna win the FA Cup,
We shall not be moved.

And it's Tottenham Hotspur,
Tottenham Hotspur FC,
They're by far the greatest team,
The world has ever seen.

Wem-ber-ley, Wem-ber-ley,
We're the famous Arsenal,
And we're going to Wem-ber-ley.

Wem-ber-ley, Wem-ber-ley,
Oh we're all pissed up,
And we're gonna win the cup.

Que sera, sera,
Whatever will be will be,
We're going to Wem-ber-ley,
Que sera, sera.

We're on the march we're Fergie's Army,
We're all going to Wem-ber-ley,
And we'll really shake them up,
When we win the FA Cup,
'Cause United are the greatest football team.

> The ubiquitous songs of victory, variations of which
> are heard at every ground in Britain.

You fill up my senses,
Like a gallon of Magnet,
Like a packet of Woodbines,
Like a good pinch of snuff.
Like a night out in Sheffield,
Like a greasy chip buttie,
Oh Sheffield United
Come thrill me again.

> 'The Greasy Chip Buttie Song', performed to the tune of John Denver's 'Annie's
> Song', as sung at Bramall Lane, Sheffield. The second line refers to a local ale.

We are the lads from The Tilton,
We'll support you till the end of the day.
We're so happy following The Blues,
We love you, what more can we say?

> A salute to the Birmingham City side of Trevor Francis, Bob Latchford, Roger Hynd
> and the late Trevor Hockey, this Seventies chant was started in the Tilton Stand at
> St. Andrew's and later immortalised on disc by the Colin Phillips Combo.

Come along the Rangers,
Buckle up you belts.
You'll maybe beat the Hearts,
But you'll never beat the Celts.

> A Parkhead rebuke to Celtic's city rivals from Ibrox.

Blackpool, Blackpool,
Blackpool by the sea.
Blackpool, Blackpool,
A place of history.
We'll follow you forever,
No matter where you go.
And when you score,
You'll hear us roar… Blackpool!

> From the Golden Mile to Bloomfield Road…
> sun, sand and soccer by the sea.

You are my Everton
My only Everton
You make me happy
When skies are grey…

> Very popular in the glory days of the mid 1980s, the Goodison Park
> edition of 'You are my Sunshine' prompted the title of the Evertonian
> fanzine *When Skies are Grey*.

Oh I am a Liverpudlian,
And I come from the Spion Kop,
I love to sing, I love to shout,
I get thrown out quite a lot.
We support the team that's dressed in red,
It's a team that you all know,
It's a team that we call Liverpool,
And to glory we will go.

> The Liverpudlian folk anthem 'Poor Scouser Tommy' as sung at Anfield.
> A traditional song based on the last words of a local soldier killed in
> North Africa, it contains the first mention of the Kop in verse.

Glory, glory, Tottenham Hotspur,
Glory, glory, Tottenham Hotspur,
Glory, glory, Tottenham Hotspur,
And the Spurs go marching on, on, on!

> Recently adopted at Old Trafford, the 'Hallelujah' Chorus was originally
> a soundtrack to the Tottenham Double during the 1960-61 season.

I want to be in that number,
When the Saints go marching in.

> No big surprises from 'The Saints' of Southampton.

Let's all sing together,
Play up sky blues,
While we sing together,
We will never lose.

> 'The Eton Boating Song', always a big Highfield Road choice: Saxophone
> solo by Sky Blues striker and keen musician Dion Dublin optional.

Good old Arsenal,
We're proud to sing that name,
While we sing this song,
We'll win the game.

> Sung to the tune of 'Rule Britannia', this was the Highbury anthem
> from May 1971 onwards.

Blue is the colour,
Football is the game,
We're all together,
And winning is our aim...

> From February 1972 onwards, the Stamford Bridge equivalent.

With an N and an E and a Wubble-U-C,
An A and an S and a T-L-E,
A U-N-I and a T-E-D,
Newcastle United, FC!

> The official St James's Park guide to spelling.

Follow, follow, we will follow Rangers,
Anywhere, everywhere, we will follow on,
Follow, follow, we will follow Rangers,
If they go to Dublin, we will follow on

> 'Follow, Follow', a Glaswegian speciality and the Ibrox Park anthem.

H-E-A-R-T-S,
If you cannot spell it, then here's what it says:
Hearts, Hearts, glorious Hearts,
It's down at Tynecastle they bide,
The talk of the toon are the boys in maroon,
And Auld Reekie supports them with pride.

'The Hearts Song', still one of the most stirring in Scottish football.

Oh it's a grand old team to play for,
It's a grand old team to see,
And if, you know, their history,
It's enough to make your heart glow (whoah-oah-
   oah-oah)
We don't care what the other team say,
What the hell do we care,
'Cause we only know that there's gonna be a show,
And the Glasgow Celtic will be there.

Also heard at Old Trafford and White Hart Lane, 'The Celtic Song'
is first and foremost the Parkhead anthem.

I sing of a team that fills me with pride,
The name of the team is the Bully Wee Clyde.
Of all Scottish teams they are dearest to me,
They've won everywhere from Dumfries to
   Dundee.

Nicknamed 'The Bully Wee', Clyde produced Scotland players such as Pat
Nevin and Steve Archibald. The club recently moved from Shawfield to
Cumbernauld, but retain strong associations with their old songs.

SHA LA LA LA LEE

All together boys,
One-two-three,
Let your voices ring!

One of the earliest reported chants hailed from Vale Park,
home of Port Vale, 1919.

Oh me lads, you should have seen us ganning,
Passing the folks along the road just as they were
    stanning,
All the lads and lasses there, all with smiling faces,
Ganning along the Scotswood Road to see the
    Blaydon Races.

Written late last century, 'Blaydon Races' has been associated with
Newcastle United since the 1920s.

On the ball, City,
Never mind the danger,
Steady on, now's your chance,
Hurrah, we've scored a goal.

Written at the turn of the century for another team in the
region, 'On the Ball City' has become a distinctive East Anglian
anthem for Norwich City.

Lucky, Lucky Arsenal!

A well-worn cry that has littered games since the 1930s, when
Herbert Chapman's Highbury dynasty first dominated English football
with cagey but tactically-astute counter-attacking football.

Play up, Pompey,
Pompey, Play up.

The 'Pompey Chimes' were initially heard in the late 1940s and
supplied a backing track to the two Division One titles won at
Fratton Park in 1949 and 1950.

Keep right on to the end of the road,
Keep right on to the end,
Though the way be long, let your heart be strong,
Keep right on round the bend.
If you're tired and weary, still journey on,
Till you come to your happy abode,
Where all you love and you're dreaming of,
Will be there at the end of the road.

Written decades earlier and originally sung by Scottish vocalist Sir Harry Lauder,
'The End of the Road' was taken up by Birmingham City fans in the 1950s and
remains one of English football's more enduring anthems.

Oh, Hampden in the sun,
Celtic seven, the Rangers one,
All my days I will sing in praise,
Of the Celtic team who played that day.

Celtic fans celebrate their high-scoring win over Rangers in the
1957-58 Scottish League Cup final.

Bra-sil, cha-cha-cha!
Bra-sil, cha-cha-cha!

Long before 'samba soccer' became one of world football's clichés, the 1962
World Cup in Chile was illuminated by the cha-chas of eventual champions Brazil.

Dead Fred, ha-ha-ha.

> The Anfield Kop revel in the misfortune of Everton striker
> Fred Pickering, who was stretchered off in a Merseyside
> derby during the early 1960s.

Two-four-six-eight,
Who do we appreciate?

> In addition to the imported 'cha-cha-chas', homegrown skipping
> rhymes were common in the late 1950s and early 1960s.

London Bridge is falling down,
Falling down, falling down,
London Bridge is falling down,
Poor old Chelsea.
Build it up with red and white,
Red and white, red and white,
Build it up with red and white,
Poor old Chelsea.

> Liverpool fans modified nursery rhymes to taunt
> London rivals Chelsea.

Go back to Italy,
Go back to Italy.

> Liverpool's first European Cup semi-final ended in aggregate defeat at the
> hands of Internazionale of Milan in 1965, but not before the Kop had
> used the 'Santa Lucia' tune to make the Italians unwelcome at Anfield.

Georgie Best, superstar,
Looks like a woman and he wears a bra.

> Patently untrue, but sung with gusto by opposing fans to the tune of
> 'Jesus Christ, Superstar' whenever Manchester United were in town.

Sha-la-la-la, Summerbee!

> The chorus of the Small Faces' classic 1966 mod anthem 'Sha La La
> La Lee' was an inspiration to Manchester City fans who sang the
> praises of flying winger Mike Summerbee.

Who the fucking hell is he?

> To the same Small Faces' tune, the Manchester United fans' reply ...

The greatest winger in history!

United one, City three!

> ... and two final retorts from the Maine Road choristers.

What are we living for?
To see Port Vale in Division Four.

> Stoke City fans looked to another 1966 hit, 'Dead End Street' by the
> Kinks, in wishing relegation turmoil on their Potteries rivals.

Where's yer handbag!

> While visiting goalkeepers were often applauded by the Kop, the
> above greeting would also occasionally come into play.

Aye-aye-aye, Charlton is better than Pelé.

> Old Trafford salutes one of its football legends.

In the town where I was born,
There is a team we go to see,
First we have ten pints of ale,
Then we go and see the Vale,
We all piss in a red and white pot,
A red and white pot, a red and white pot.
We all piss in a red and white pot,
A red and white pot, a red and white pot.

> The Beatles' 1966 hit 'Yellow Submarine' surfaced in many guises
> on the terraces in the 1960s, this Port Vale version suggesting an
> alternative use for the colours of local rivals Stoke City.

We all live in a blue and white Kop,
A blue and white Kop, a blue and white Kop.

> Sheffield Wednesday fans used the same song to honour
> Hillsborough's own Spion Kop. The tune was also very popular — in
> its original form — at Norwich City, a team who play in yellow shirts.

Their eyes they shine like diamonds,
They are the best team in the land,
And there was Billy Bremner,
Stood there with the Cup in his hand.

Leeds United fans celebrated their 1968 League Cup win over Arsenal
at Wembley with this version of 'Black Velvet Band', a chart hit the
previous year for the Dubliners.

Hello, hello, we are the Busby Boys,
Hello, hello, we are the Busby Boys,
And if you are a City fan, surrender or you'll die,
For we will follow United.

An Old Trafford favourite.

When the red, red robin,
Comes bob, bob, bobbing along,
Shoot the bastard, shoot the bastard!
Shoot, shoot, shoot!

The anthem of Charlton Athletic — and a number of other teams who
play in red shirts, such as Swindon Town — as sung by opposition fans.

Who's that team they call the Rangers,
Who's that team they all adore.
We're the boys in royal blue,
And we're Scotland's gallant crew,
And we're out to show the world what we can do.

An Ibrox anthem ...

Hail, hail Celtic, sing we proudly,
Hail, hail Celtic, sing we all,
Glasgow, Scottish and League Cup,
Celtic, they will pick them up,
And they'll prove themselves the champions of
them all.

... and a Parkhead variation on the theme.

From the banks of the River Irvine
To the shores of Sicily.
We'll fight, fight, fight for the Killie,
Till we win the Scottish League.

A Rugby park chant that would seem preposterous in the 1990s, which have been dominated by Glasgow's Old Firm. In the 1960s, however, it was different and Kilmarnock won the Scottish title, and gained entry into the following year's European Cup, in 1965. From the town of Dumfries, the Queen of the South version of the same song opened with 'from the bonny, bonny banks of the River Nith, to the shores of Tripoli'.

YOU'RE SUPPOSED TO BE AT HOME

Taunts, aspersions and insults

We all agree,
Banks is better than Yashin,
Dobing's better than Eusébio,
And United are in for a thrashing.

> A warning to Manchester United from fans of a Stoke City side containing goalkeeper Gordon Banks and striker Peter Dobing, twin lynchpins of the 1972 League Cup winning team. The Soviet goalkeeper Lev Yashin and Portuguese striker Eusébio were both European Footballers of the Year in the Sixties.

Oh I do like to be beside the seaside,
Oh I do like to be beside the sea,
Oh I do like to walk along the prom, prom, prom,
Where the brass band plays 'Fuck Off West Brom'.

> 'Oh, I Do Like To Be Beside The Seaside', as sung by rival fans to the pride of The Hawthorns.

And it's no nay never, no nay never no more,
'Til we play bastard Rovers, no never, no more

> The Burnley adaptation of the traditional song 'The Wild Rover', as sung to their East Lancashire rivals Blackburn.

Come in a taxi,
You must have come in a taxi.

> Traditional greeting, to the tune of 'Guantanamera', to an away side with meagre support.

Come in a Jiffi,
You must have come in a Jiffi.

> The safe-sex variant of the above chant, a Jiffi being a well-known
> brand of condom.

They're turning Highbury into a public lavatory,
They're turning Highbury into a public lavatory,
They're turning Highbury into a public lavatory,
So we can all piss up the wall.

> Tottenham fans adapt their own 'Glory, Glory Hallelujah' anthem
> to spice up the North London derby . . .

And a spoonful of Sugar helps the Tottenham go down,
Tottenham go down, Tottenham go down.
And a spoonful of Sugar helps the Tottenham go down,
In a most delightful way.

> . . . and the Arsenal hordes reply with a little help from 'Mary Poppins',
> the Sugar in question being the Tottenham chairman Alan.

He's a bald-headed bastard dressed in black,
Dressed in black, dressed in black,
Dressed in boo-bah black,
Every time we score a goal, he says no,
Every time we score a goal, he says no.
'Cause he's a bald-headed bastard dressed in black,
Dressed in black, dressed in black,
Dressed in boo-bah black.

> Leeds fans looked to Mungo Jerry's 1974 hit 'Long Legged Woman Dressed
> In Black' for a chant in which the referee was their adversary.

The referee's a wanker.

The referee's a toilet.

Who's the bastard in the black?

> Traditional chiding of the referee.

Who's the bastard in the green?

> Traditional chiding of the referee after the Premiership
> led to a change in the colours of the officials' kits.

Linesman, linesman,
You're such a farce.
Why don't you stick that flag,
Right up your fucking arse,

> The men who run the line also come under attention.

Up your arse, right up your arse,
Stick your blue flag up your arse,
From Stamford Bridge to Upton Park,
Stick your blue flag up your arse.

> West Ham fans volley 'The Blue Flag' back at Chelsea.

We hate Nottingham Forest,
We hate Liverpool too,
We hate Man United,
But Chelsea we love you.

> Sung to the tune of 'Land Of Hope And Glory', this litany of loathed
> clubs was usually prefaced with a loud *all together now*.

Bye-bye, Harry Catterick, bye-bye,
You're going to the Second Division, goodbye,
All those Koppites drinking whiskey and rye,
Singing this will be the day that you die.

> Liverpool fans used Don McLean's 1972 epic for a tune to
> taunt Mersey rivals Everton and Harry Catterick, their man-
> ager of the Sixties and early Seventies.

Supermac, Superstar.
How many goals have you scored so far?

> Newcastle striker Malcolm Macdonald's scoring record
> often came under scrutiny, to the tune of 'Jesus Christ,
> Superstar', from rival fans.

He's fat, he's round,
He's taken Leicester down.

> Reading fans delighted in the fact that former manager Mark
> McGhee, who agreed that he was slightly overweight, took new club
> Leicester City down to Division One from the Premiership in the
> 1994-95 season.

Where were you when you were shit?

> Sung to Blackburn fans during their team's 1994-95 champi-
> onship year, the implication being that the club's increased sup-
> port was due only to shallow glory-hunters.

If Shearer plays for England, so can I!

> Spurs fans, misguided in the extreme, taunted Blackburn Rovers striker
> Alan Shearer with this taunt in December 1995, mocking his blank run
> at international level. Later in the same game Shearer struck the
> winning goal, his hundredth in the Premiership, from 25 yards.

Shit on The Villa,
Shit on The Villa tonight!

> Sung by Birmingham City fans to the tune of 'Roll Out The Barrel',
> this traditional West Midlands greeting is reserved for their Villa Park
> rivals. It also emblazoned midfielder Paul Tait's chest during the
> 1994-95 Auto Windscreens Shield Final at Wembley. Tait lifted his
> club colours to reveal the slogan on a T-shirt after scoring the winner.

Birmingham, are you listening,
To the song that we're singing?
We're walking along, singing a song,
Shitting on the City as we go.

> To the tune of 'Winter Wonderland', the Aston Villa response.

Piss in your water, we're gonna piss in your water.

> Sung to Leeds fans in 1995 by a Newcastle crowd. It was at
> the time of an operation to ship water from their region to
> drought-stricken Yorkshire.

You're supposed to be at home!

> To the tune of the Welsh hymn 'Bread Of Heaven', this refrain
> is sung by away fans at a home crowd who are either losing
> heavily or are unable to find their singing voice. It was,
> however, also sung to Dutch supporters by England fans in Euro
> 96 when the Wembley scoreboard showed 'Netherlands 1,
> England 4', even though England were the home side.

Can we play you every week?

> Bolton fans, as their team end a long barren run by winning 4-1
> away at Middlesbrough. The chant, to the tune of 'Bread Of
> Heaven' was often echoed by Everton fans in the Mersey derby.
> Despite struggling in the Nineties, the Goodison side always
> raised their game against Liverpool.

Why are your pies so shit?
> Burnley fans comment on the cuisine at Swansea's
> Vetch field in 1983.

RODNEY, RODNEY
WE LOVE YOU

We're one of those teams that you see now and then,
We often score six, but we seldom score ten,
We beat them at home and we beat them away,
We kill any bastard that gets in our way
We're the pride of all Europe, the cock of the north
We hate the Scousers, the Cockneys, of course
    (and Leeds!)
We are United without any doubt,
We are the Manchester boys.
La-la-la, la-la-la-la-la ...'

> One of the classic Manchester United anthems, sung to the tune of
> 'One Of Those Songs'

Underneath the floodlights,
Down in Dusseldorf,
All the Kopites singing,
Bevvied up of course.
We've been to Lisbon, and to Rome,
And our team never walks alone,
We're going back to Wembley,
To bring the cup back home.

> The Anfield version of 'Lili Marlene', sung in the build-up
> to the European Cup Final of 1978, when Liverpool beat
> FC Brugge 1-0 at Wembley.

We ain't got a barrel of money,
But we've got Woodward and Currie.
And with Eddie Colquhoun,
Promotion will be soon, United.

> The Bramall Lane version of the standard 'Side By Side' helped to
> spur Sheffield United to promotion from Division Two in 1971.

There was a team called City,
They came from Birmingham.
They got knocked out of the FA Cup,
By Alex Stock's Fulham.

Sung by Aston Villa fans to mark the shock elimination of
their local rivals in the 1975 FA Cup Semi-Final against
Second Division Fulham. The line *'Alex Stock's Fulham'*
was amended to *'non-League Altrincham'* after Blues were
victims of another cup giant-killing in the Eighties.

Rodney, Rodney, we love you,
That's what we all think of you.

Manchester City fans acclaim Rodney Marsh to the tune of
Clive Dunn's 1970 Christmas hit 'Grandad'. Marsh's
Queen's Park Rangers soul-mate Stanley Bowles was simi-
larly canonised to Slade's 'My Friend Stan'.

Give us an assembly,
And we'll give you back your Wembley

The Tartan Army make their contribution to the devolution
debate after tearing up the Wembley turf following
Scotland's 2-1 defeat of England in June 1977.

Champions, Champions... Champions of Europe!

Elland Road cheered Don Revie's team with this call-and-
response chant, despite the fact that Leeds never actually
won the European Cup.

He shoots, he scores,
He must be Peter Ward.

> The Brighton and England striker was one of many forwards
> acclaimed to the strains of 'The Quartermaster's Store'.

In your Liverpool slums,
In your Liverpool slums,
You look in the dustbin for something to eat,
You find a dead cat and you think it's a treat,
In your Liverpool slums.

> Unsubtle and derogatory songs about the north, such as this mutation
> of 'My Liverpool Home', were common among fans of the supposed-
> ly more sophisticated and cosmopolitan London clubs.

Willie, Willie Morgan
Willie Morgan on the wing.

> Manchester United's wing wizard, one of the first to be tagged 'The New George
> Best', was applauded to the tune of 'Gin Gan Goolie', a 1970 hit for The Scaffold.

Do not be mistaken,
Do not be misled,
We are not Scousers,
We're from Birkenhead.
You can keep you cathedral,
And Pier Head,
We are not Scousers,
We're from Birkenhead.

> Prenton Park regulars were keen to assert Tranmere's autonomy from
> the sights and soccer teams of nearby Liverpool.

Oh this year, we're gonna win the Cup,
Y viva el Fulham,
And next year you know we're going up,
Y viva el Fulham.

> Sylvia's 1974 holiday hit 'Y Viva Espana' inspired both a
> saucy reggae hit in Judge Dread's 'Y Viva Suspenders' and
> Fulham's terrace song for the 1975 FA Cup Final.

Allez les vertes!

> Or 'come on you greens'. Sung by supporters of St
> Etienne (the French team rather than the Nineties dance
> act) the chant also appealed to fans of Celtic, who were
> exposed to it before the 1976 European Cup Final
> between the Frenchmen and Bayern Munich in Glasgow.

Come on without,
Come on within,
You ain't see nothing,
Like the mighty Emlyn.

Stevie Heighway's always running,
Johnny Toshack's always scoring,
Can you hear the Koppites roaring,
Toshack is our King.

> Anfield legends acclaimed in two Seventies chants, the
> first to the sound of Manfred Mann's number one single
> 'The Mighty Quinn', the second to the more traditional
> 'Sons Of Harlech'.

Born is the King of White Hart Lane.

A Tottenham favourite, earmarked for striker Alan Gilzean in the early part of the decade and midfielder Glenn Hoddle in the latter part.

Na-na-na-na, Na-na-na-na, Hey-hey, Tottenham Hotspur.

Covered by Bananarama in the Eighties, Steam's 1970 single 'Na Na Hey Hey Kiss Him Goodbye' was also a hit at White Hart Lane...

We are Tottenham, we are Tottenham, We are Tottenham, from the Lane.

... as was Rod Stewart's 'Sailing' ...

Power to the Park Lane, Power to the Park Lane, Power to the Park Lane, Power to the Park Lane - right on!

... and, in the Park Lane Stand, 'Power To The People' by John Lennon and The Plastic Ono Band.

All we are saying, is give us a goal.

An altered version of Lennon's 'Give Peace A Chance' was also widely popular.

We will follow the Chelsea
Over land and sea… and Leicester!
We will follow the Chelsea
Onto victory.

> Sung to 'Land Of Hope And Glory'. Quite why Leicester is reckoned not to
> be of 'land and sea' is one of the great mysteries of football chanting.

Proud Posh or Pompey,
Notts County or anyone,
We'll sing together,
Until the game is won.

> Much the same goes for a Leeds song from the Seventies which
> lists Peterborough, Portsmouth and Notts County as rivals during
> an era in which Elland Road hosted the more illustrious likes of
> Celtic and Barcelona in Europe.

Who put the ball in the West Ham net?
Skip to my Lou Macari.

> Old Trafford commemorates one of Lou Macari's first Manchester
> United goals, against West Ham United in 1973.

Oh Arthur, Arthur,
Arthur, Arthur, Arthur, Arthur Albiston.

> Chicory Tip's 'Son Of My Father' provided a basis for the exaltation
> of an Old Trafford utility man.

We're on our way to Roma,
On the 25th of May,
All the Koppites will be singing,
Vatican bells, they will be ringing,
Liverpool FC will be singing,
When we win the European Cup.

Liverpool fans sing up for the European Cup. Inspired by Kevin Keegan,
they beat German champions Borussia Mönchengladbach in Rome
to win the trophy for the first time in May 1977.

Oh come all ye faithful, joyful and triumphant,
Oh come ye, Oh come ye, to Anfield,
Come and behold them, we're the kings of Europe,
Oh come let us behold them, oh come let us
    behold them,
Oh come let us behold them, Liverpool.

The trophy won, Anfield acclaimed its returning European heroes.

Bobby Latchford, Bobby Latchford,
Hero of The Blues,
Bobby Latchford, Bobby Latchford,
King of Saint Andrews.

Birmingham City fans pay tribute to the spearhead of their attack.

Brown shit on the pitch,
Tra-la-la-la-lee.

Boney M's 'Brown Girl In The Ring' was the inspiration to Chelsea fans
who gave an ardent thumbs down to Coventry City's all-brown away kit.

Score, Arsenal, score,
Once you get one you'll get more.
We'll sing your assembly when we get to Wembley,
So score, Arsenal, score.

A familiar refrain at Highbury during the Seventies.

No-one likes us, no-one likes us,
No-one likes us, we don't care.
We are Millwall, super Millwall,
We are Millwall, from The Den.

Rod Stewart's 'Sailing' was the tune for this Millwall anthem. A
reported Birmingham City version of the same song substituted the
phrase 'we're a bit concerned' at the end of the second line.

WE'LL SEE YOU ALL OUTSIDE

Oggy-oggy-oggy, oi-oi-oi!
Oggy-oggy-oggy! oi-oi-oi!
Oggy, oi! Oggy, oi!
Oggy-oggy-oggy,oi-oi-oi!
Zigger-zagger, zigger-zagger,
Shut your mouth!

Non-specific hooligan-era chant.

You're gonna get your fucking heads kicked in.

You're going home in a London ambulance.

You're going home in a black and white ambulance.

You're going home in a military ambulance.

The aggro-merchants often made their rivals an offer of transport home. The first chant was heard everywhere, the second originated in London, the third in Newcastle and the fourth in Swindon, as home fans taunted Bolton supporters during the national ambulance-men's dispute of 1989. The 'military' line alludes to the army vehicles on standby in the dispute.

Hoolie, hoolie, hooligan!
Hoolie, hooligan!

A hoodlum's battle-cry, based on the single 'Helule, Helule', a chart hit for the Tremeloes in 1968.

Park Lane, Park Lane, do your job,
Park Lane, do your job.

'Helule, Helule' was again the inspiration behind this chant, an
internal Tottenham affair. The 'job' in question was that of
giving the away fans a chasing, the Shelf and Paxton Road
stands at White Hart Lane imploring those in the Park Lane —
closest to the away fans — to complete the task.

Those were the days, my friend,
We took the Stretford End,
We took the Shed, the Northbank Highbury,
We took the Geordies too,
We fight for Liverpool,
We are the Kop, from Liverpool FC.

We are the Shed, my friend,
We took the Stretford End,
We'll sing and dance and do it all again,
We live the life we choose,
We fight and never lose,
We are The Shed, oh yes we are The Shed.

Two versions of Mary Hopkin's 1968 number one hit 'Those Were
The Days', the first from Liverpool, the second from Chelsea. The
song later provided the basis for the familiar chant of 'we'll see you
all outside' and, in 1978, was aired as 'we want our money back'
by disgruntled Scotland fans at the World Cup in Argentina.

We'll fight with no surrender,
We'll fight for the boys in red,
We'll fight, we'll fight for Liverpool,
The team that Shankly bred.

Victorious,
And glorious,
We'll take Gladwys Street,
Between the four of us.

Two Anfield battle cries, the second predicting trouble in the Gladwys
Street Stand of rivals Everton and implying that a quartet of Liverpool
fans would be enough to secure a hooligan foothold on enemy turf.

Tip toe through the Spion Kop,
With your pumps on,
Sucking a lollipop,
Tip toe through the Spion Kop with me.

One of the many Everton retorts – this one sung to the tune of 'Tip
Toe Through the Tulips' – reserved for visits to Anfield.

Tip toe through the Kippax,
With a flick knife,
And a sawn-off shotgun,
Tip toe through the Kippax with me.

A more sinister-rounding serenade to local rivals City from
Manchester United fans. The Kippax Stand runs along one
side of City's Maine Road stadium.

Captain Jack, Captain Jack,
Meet me by the railway track,
With a bottle in my hand,
I wanna be your fighting man.

Queen's Park Rangers get in on the act.

We've got the whole West Stand in our hands,
We've got the whole West Stand in our hands,
We've got the whole West Stand in our hands,
We've got the whole stand in our hands,

Sung by Spurs fans after they had pushed past police lines and into the
home section of the West Stand at Coventry City's Highfield Road in the
1970-71 season. As reported in *The Glory Game* by Hunter Davies.

Hark now, hear the Arsenal sing,
The Tottenham run away,
And we will fight forevermore,
Because of Boxing Day.

Seasonal cheer from the Northbank at Highbury. Sung to the
Christmas carol 'Hark The Herald Angels Sing', the song dates back
to a tradition of local derbies on the morning of Boxing Day.

He's only a poor little Gunner,
His face is all tattered and torn,
He made me feel sick,
So I hit him with a brick,
And now he don't sing anymore.

Spurs supporters transformed the dainty sentiments of 'The Sparrow',
a 1979 hit for The Ramblers.

We had joy, we had fun,
We had Tottenham on the run,
But the joy didn't last,
'Cause the bastards ran too fast.

A popular chant all over the land, this was sung to the tune of
'Seasons In The Sun', a number one hit in 1974 for Terry Jacks.

My old man said be an Arsenal fan,
I said 'fuck off, bollocks, you're a c**t!',
We took the Northbank in half a minute,
We took The Shed with the Chelsea in it,
The Hammers we hammered,
With chisels and spanners,
We taught the Arsenal bastards how to run,
You can never trust a Gunner,
'Cause the Gunners are runners,
When they fight with T. H. F. C.

> Judging by the second line, a very dysfunctional father-son relationship was under consideration here. Sung to the tune of 'Follow The Van', this song appeared in slightly changed form at most London clubs. It also surely holds the record for the most expletives in a single line. As sung by Spurs fans, the middle section once ran 'you name it, we've won it. The Double we've done it, we've never lost a match at Wem-ber-ley'. This was, of course, before they were humbled by Coventry City in the 1987 Cup Final.

I'm a knock-kneed chicken, I'm a bow-legged hen,
I haven't been so happy since I don't know when.
I walk with a wiggle and a waddle and a squawk,
Doing the Liverpool boot walk.

> The Anfield celebration of 'The Tennessee Wig Walk' was big during the Seventies ...

I was walking down Shoreham Street singing a song,
Along came a pig fan and asked what's wrong.
I kicked him in the balls and I kicked him in the
     head,
Now that Wednesday fan is dead.

> ... as was the Sheffield United version of the same song ...

We hate Bill Shankly and we hate the Kop,
We'll fight Man United until we drop,
We don't give a wiggle and we don't give a wank,
We are the Highbury… Northbank!

> … and an Arsenal variation on the theme.

I asked Don Revie and Bertie Mee,
Have you heard of the Northbank, Highbury?
They both said no, I don't think so
But I've heard of the North Stand aggro!

> Slightly eccentric, in that Bertie Mee was actually manager of
> Arsenal, but popular at Stamford Bridge in the Seventies.

United sing, I don't know why,
Perhaps they just want to die.

> Based on 'Tom Hark', a hit for The Piranhas in 1980, this
> Manchester City chant was relatively short and to the point.

We hate Bill Shankly and we hate St John,
But most of all we hate Big Ron,
And we'll hang the Koppites one by one,
On the banks of the royal blue Mersey.
To hell with Liverpool and Rangers too,
We'll throw them all in the Mersey,
And we'll fight, fight, fight with all our might,
For the boys in the royal blue jerseys.

> Everton supporters voice distaste for Liverpool fans and star players
> Ian St John and Ron Yeats.

Don't cry for me Aston Villa,
The truth is I cannot stand you.
All through my wild days,
My mad existence.
We took The Holte End,
Without resistance.

The spirit of *Evita* was alive and well at St. Andrew's in the Seventies
as Birmingham City fans unveiled their version of Julie Covington's
1976 hit 'Don't Cry For Me Argentina'.

WE'LL TAKE
GOOD CARE OF YOU

We've got Mirandinha,
He's not from Argentina,
He's from Brazil,
And he's fucking brill!

> The Toon Army rejoiced in the arrival of Brazilian
> striker Mirandinha at St James's Park ...

We've got Kenny Wharton,
He's not from Bishop Auckland.
He's from Cowgate,
And he's fucking great.

> ... but also found time to acclaim an unsung hero from closer to
> home. An alternate climax to the latter chant was 'he's from The
> Toon, and he's drinking Broon'.

Oh lucky, lucky,
Lucky, lucky, lucky Liverpool.

> Crystal Palace fans looking on the bright side, to the tune of Chicory
> Tip's 'Son Of My Father', during a 9-0 defeat at Anfield in 1989.

We went down to the Bridge, we needed a win,
And Kenny put the ball in the net.
It's sixteen, it's beautiful,
And it's mine.

> Liverpool win the First Division championship for a record sixteenth
> time, to the tune of 'You're Sixteen', a goal from Kenny Dalglish giv-
> ing them a 1-0 win away Stamford Bridge in 1986.

Yippie-yi-yo, yippie-yi-yay,
Holte Enders in the sky.

Aston Villa fans delight in the awesome height of Villa Park's
massive Holte End. The tune is 'Ghost Riders In The Sky'.

You'll never beat Des Walker.

Nottingham Forest fans took great solace from the imperious form of
their English international centre-back during the Eighties.

We all agree, Des Walker's worth more than Derby.

Forest fans at the time of the proposed sale of local
rivals Derby County.

He's fat, he's round,
He bounces on the ground.

Liverpool fans consider the stocky frame of Sammy Lee.

Sammy Lee, Sammy Lee.

Liverpool fans again, this time after a particularly
stocky infant in a red top had run onto the pitch to
get the ball in a derby match with Everton.

We'll take good care of you,
Archibald, Archibald.

> Tottenham fans fly the flag and borrow a line from a well-
> known British Airways advert to salute their Scottish striker
> in the 1981 FA Cup Final.

Archibald, oh! Archibald, oh!
Archibald is something to be scared of.

> At Wembley again the following year, the Spurs supporters adapt
> the 'ridicule is nothing to be scared of' line from the hit 'Prince
> Charming' by Adam And The Ants.

Stevie Foster, Stevie Foster,
What a difference you have made.

> Manchester United fans adapt 'Bread Of Heaven' at Wembley in hon-
> our of Brighton's headbanded centre-half in the replay of the 1983
> FA Cup Final. Foster missed the original game, a 2-2 draw, through
> suspension. He returned for the replay, which Brighton lost 4-0.

Let him die, let him die, let him die.

> Manchester United regulars convey their sympathies to a Tottenham
> goalkeeper, stretched off in an FA Cup Third Round Replay at Old Trafford in 1980.

Two World Wars, one World Cup, doo-dah, doo-dah.

> England fans, in Germany for the 1988 European Championship.

Two Gary Stevens,
There's only two Gary Stevens.

> England fans sang an unusual variation of 'Guantanamera' in the
> 1986 World Cup, their squad containing two defenders with the
> same name, one an Everton player and the other a Spurs one.

Ireland's, Ireland's number one.

> A Kop greeting for Manchester United goalkeeper Gary
> Bailey after his error had given the Republic Of Ireland a
> Wembley goal against England.

How would you like to be?
A Scouser in Gay Paree,
Walking along on the banks of the Seine,
Winning the European Cup once again,
We went up the Eiffel Tower,
But only for half-an-hour,
We won't be late, to celebrate,
Our victory in Gay Paree.

> Liverpool fans in Paris for the European Cup Final against
> Real Madrid in May 1981.

Alan Cork, Alan Cork,
Alan, Alan Cork,
He's got no hair, and we don't care,
Alan, Alan Cork!

> Wimbledon fans acclaim their follicly-challenged striker.

Tottenham, Tottenham,
Can you hear us on the box?

A familiar refrain, to the tune of 'Bread Of Heaven', at televised
matches in the Eighties.

Stayed in your wine bar,
You should have stayed in your wine bar.

Tottenham fans with mock sympathy to Watford's stand-in goalkeeper, a part-
time player who also ran a wine bar, in the 1987 FA Cup Semi-Final at Villa
Park. The tune used was 'Guantanamera' and Spurs won 4-1.

Red army, red army, red army, red army ...

A Highbury refrain.

Who ate all the pies?
Who ate all the pies?
You fat bastard, you fat bastard,
You ate all the pies!

General chant to the tune of 'Knees Up Mother Brown'.

We are the nutters who live by the sea.

Fans of Southport, who lost their Football League place to Wigan
Athletic in 1978, assert a degree of craziness.

**Score in a minute,
We're gonna score in a minute.**

> The traditional chant in support of a side who are
> dominating the play and threatening a goal ...

**Score in a brothel,
You couldn't score in a brothel.**

> ... and the traditional riposte.

**Sing, sing, wherever you may be,
We are the famous CFC,
And we don't give a fuck, wherever we may be,
'Cause we are the famous CFC.**

> Traditional folk hymn 'The Lord Of The Dance',
> as sung at Stamford Bridge.

**Sing, sing, wherever you may be,
We lost the League Cup at Wem-ber-ley,
But we'll be back to win the other three,
And we'll go down in history.**

> Spurs fans try to look on the bright side after a 3-1 defeat
> by Liverpool in the 1982 League Cup Final. At the time,
> the North London side were still in the running for three
> other trophies. They ended up with just the FA Cup.

We are top of the league!
I said, We are top of the league!

Ooh-Aah, Paul McGrath!
I Said, Ooh-Aah, Paul McGrath!

Ooh-Aah, Lineker!
I Said, Ooh-Aah, Lineker!

Ooh-Aah, Where's the bar!
I Said, Ooh-Aah, Where's the bar!

Variations on a theme.

WE'RE NOT REALLY HERE

We're not really, we're not really here,
We're not really, we're not really here,
Just like a fan of the invisible man,
We're not really here.

> Wishful thinking from long-suffering Manchester City fans,
> to the tune of 'We Shall Not Be Moved', as their side
> struggle in Division One in 1997.

And number one is Perry Groves,
And number two is Perry Groves,
And number three is Perry Groves,
And number four is Perry Groves.
We all live in a Perry Groves world,
A Perry Groves world, a Perry Groves world.
We all live in a Perry Groves world,
A Perry Groves world, a Perry Groves world.

> Arsenal fans salute Highbury wing merchant Perry Groves with an
> eccentric rendition of 'Yellow Submarine'.

We all agree Emmerdale's better than Brookside.

> Halifax fans acclaim the perceived superiority of a
> Yorkshire soap opera over its Liverpudlian rival in an FA
> Cup tie at Marine, Merseyside in 1992.

We all agree Tiswas is better than Swapshop.

> The Kop try to enliven an unexciting Saturday afternoon at Anfield in the
> early Eighties with a debate on that morning's childrens' television.

We're on the drugs with Ally's Army,
We're all taking Benzadrine,
And we'll really shake them up,
When we drink it out of a cup,
'Cause Scotland are the greatest football team.

Scotland fans at Wembley, *Euro 96*.

I love a lassie,
A bonny, bonny lassie,
She's as thin as the paper on the wall.
Legs like a spider,
I'd like to fuckin' ride her,
Mary from Maryhill.

Partick Thistle fans — whose Firhill ground is in Maryhill, Glasgow — salute
the local female population with scant regard for political correctness.

My garden shed,
Is bigger than this.
My garden shed,
Is bigger than this.
It's got a door,
And a window.
My garden shed,
Is bigger than this.

The considered opinion of Birmingham City fans on the
state of some of the smaller stadiums visited during their
sojourn in the old Third Division. The chant is sung to the
tune of 'When The Saints Go Marching In'.

It's a heartache,
Following the Partick.

Even Bonnie Tyler, who had a hit in 1977 with 'It's A Heartache', never
knew agony or ecstasy on the scale of those who visit Firhill for thrills.

Oh Southend Pier is longer than yours,
Oh Southend Pier is longer then yours.
Its got some shops and a railway,
Oh Southend Pier is longer than yours.

Pier pressure usually tells when Roots Hall regulars taunt
the supporters of other seaside towns. Again sung to
'When The Saints Go Marching In'.

Oh when the beans come out of the tin,
Oh when the beans come out of the tin,
I want to be there by that toaster,
When the beans come out of the tin.

Newcastle United fans, to the tune of 'When The Saints Go Marching
In', look forward to an exquisite post-match meal. The refrain is one
of many recorded by local singer Harry Palmer.

Oh Sheffield is wonderful,
Oh Sheffield is wonderful,
It's got tits, fanny and the Wednesday,
Oh Sheffield is wonderful.

Sung to 'When The Saints Go Marching In'. The men of Hillsborough
apparently also love women for their minds.

I had a wheelbarrow, the wheel fell off.

Repeated over and over to the tune of 'On Top Of Old Smokey', this strange chant was kept going by Notts County fans for the entire second half of their FA Cup Fifth Round tie at Tottenham in 1991.

I've got a wheelbarrow,
The front wheel is bent.

More nonsense from the garden centre, this time from Edgeley Park, where Stockport County supporters — again to the tune of 'Old Smokey' — augmented the chant by wearing headgear consisting of blue-and-white foam wheelbarrows.

What a load of scrubbers!

Spurs fans ridicule a pre-match display of female gymnastics at Highfield Road, Coventry in the early Seventies.

Peter Shilton, Peter Shilton,
Does you missus know you're here?

The Nottingham Forest and England goalkeeper was often taunted after newspaper allegations about his private life in the Seventies.

Dicks out! Dicks out!

Fans of a struggling Fulham side took great delight in a chant calling for the dismissal of manager Alan Dicks in 1991.

Got one Pinas,
We've only got one Pinas.

> To the tune of 'Guantanamera', Newcastle United fans took great delight
> in the surname of their young Dutch player, who was on the sub's bench
> during the team's 1997-98 Champions League campaign.

His name is Ravanelli,
He's always on the telly,
Showing us his belly,
His name's Fabrizio.

> Middlesbrough supporters salute their imported Italian striker to the
> tune of 'The Addams Family'. Fabrizio Ravanelli made a habit of
> pulling his shirt over his face after scoring.

Hot dog, sausage roll,
Come on Tottenham, score a goal.

Meat pie, sausage roll,
Come on Oldham, score a goal!

> A pair of chants illustrating the differences in regional cuisine.

He's got a pineapple on his head!

> Sung to 'He's Got The Whole World In His Hands' and later picked up on
> television by Fantasy Football League, this chant was initially directed at
> winger Jamie Lawrence of Leicester City, but became renowned in 1996
> because of striker Jason Lee, then at Nottingham Forest.

Where's your monkey gone?

> Sung to the tune of Middle Of The Road's 1971 hit 'Chirpy Chirpy Cheep Cheep', this chant is often sung to the home supporters by fans visiting Hartlepool United's Victoria Park. Folklore has it that locals once hung a monkey, the only survivor of a shipwrecked Napoleonic vessel, believing it to be a French spy.

Playing number nine for you!

> To the same tune, the Hartlepool reply.

Six foot two, Eyes of blue,
Big Jim Holton's after you.

> A crowd favourite at Old Trafford and one of the epic chants of the Seventies. The odd thing here, however, is that the Manchester United and Scotland defender's were not blue, but brown.

Attack. Attack. Attack, attack, attack!

> A familiar cry as Anfield urges Liverpool to push forward.

A cat. A cat. A cat, a cat, a cat!

> The Kop lauds a feline pitch invader during the Seventies.

Where 'ast tha been since I saw thee,
At Elland Road bah t'at.

Yorkshire tradition upheld by Leeds United fans.

Kenny Burns has got a brand new motor car.

Forest fans marvel at the upwardly-mobile lifestyle of a Scottish stopper.

Armani's number one!

Liverpool fans salute the style of goalkeeper David
James, who signed a lucrative contract to model for
Italian designer Giorgio Armani in 1996.

Sing when it's snowing,
You only sing when it's snowing

The Arctic weather report, according to Chelsea fans
during a farcical snowbound away fixture against
Tromso in the European Cup-Winners' Cup in 1997.

Sing when you're fishing,
You only sing when you're fishing.

The taunt faced by fans of Grimsby Town, nicknamed
'The Mariners', has given the club's fanzine its
name, Sing When We're Fishing.

Bring me salmon in your smile,
Bring me haddock all the while.
In this world where we live,
there should be more halibut.
So much joy you can give,
To each dolphin-friendly tuna.
Bring me mackerel, through the dace,
Never bring me any plaice.
May your shark be as warm,
As the squid from up above.
Bring me sardines, bring me pilchards,
Bring me cod.

A suggested Grimsby crowd retort, based on 'Bring Me Sunshine', as
circulated in a fanzine songsheet.

Come on the fish-fish-fish-fish, Fisher,
Oh we're going to win the game today!

More fishy business from Dr Martens League side Fisher Athletic.

One man went to mow, went to mow a meadow,
One man and his dog – spot! – went to mow a
     meadow.

A particular favourite at Stamford Bridge, where the whole song is sung.

GO WEST!

Go West, Bromwich Albion!

One-nil, to the Arsenal!

Nayim, from the half way line!

You're shit and you know you are!

We're shit and we're sick of it!

You're merde and you know you are!

We're shit, but we won four-one!

We're beef and we're proud of it!

Eight variations on the 'Go West' theme. The single, once a hit for the Village People, was revived by the Pet Shop Boys in 1993 and has since spawned a spate of chants. The third variation here refers to Spanish player Nayim's 50-yard winning goal against Arsenal in the Final of the 1995 European Cup-Winners' Cup. The fifth variation was sung by disgruntled Manchester City fans, the sixth by Aston Villa supporters in Bordeaux during a UEFA Cup tie, the seventh by Torquay United fans celebrating an away win over Brighton in 1998. The final permutation was sung by Leeds fans amid furore over the rise of mad cow disease.

It's just like watching Brazil.

The refrain, to the tune of 'Blue Moon', that accompanied Barnsley's
rise to the Premiership in 1997.

It's just like watching The Bill.

It's just like watching Grange Hill.

Retorts from opposition fans, the first from Chelsea and
the second from Derby Country.

It's just like watching Rye Hill.

Barnsley fans turn the chant back on themselves during a
heavy defeat away at Oxford United in 1997. Rye Hill is a
village outside Barnsley.

It's just like watching Man U.

The Old Trafford faithful taunt the Barnsley supporters in a
7-0 victory in 1997.

Five-four, we're gonna win five-four.

The chant, still to the tune of 'Blue Moon', of the Barnsley supporters
at half-time in the above match. Their side was already 4-0 down.

We want ten! We want ten!

Manchester United fans taunt relegation-threatened Ipswich Town as
their team strolls to to a 9-0 victory at Old Trafford in 1995.

We want one! We want one!

The riposte from the Ipswich fans.

Three-nil, we only lost three-nil.

Ipswich fans celebrate a comparatively narrow defeat against
Tottenham in their next match.

Super, super John, super, super John,
Super, super John, super John McGinlay.

The Bolton Wanderers faithful immortalise their Scottish striker.

We're walking along, singing a song,
Walking in a Shearer wonderland.

Blackburn Rovers honour Super Al. The chant was also sung in praise
of Jürgen Klinsmann at Tottenham.

Now we are the world's most passionate fans,
And we look real cool, 'cause the Geordies rule,
With Ginola, la-la-la Ginola,
He'll score us a goala.
She walked up to me and she asked me to dance,
I said 'get lost Mackem, I'm from France',
I'm Ginola, la-la-la Ginola,
He'll score us a goala.

The Toon Army praise their brilliant French winger and ridicule their local 'Mackem' rivals from Sunderland, all to the tune of 'Lola', a hit in 1970 for The Kinks.

Andy Cole, Andy Cole,
Andy, Andy Cole,
He gets the ball and scores a goal,
Andy, Andy Cole.

Originally sung by Newcastle United fans in tribute to 'Goal King' Cole, this chant was thrown back to the Toon Army with the third line amended to 'he gets the ball and does fuck all'.

The referee's a Geordie.

You're balls don't bounce enough.

Two chants directed at the Toon Army by supporters of GM Vauxhall Conference side Stevenage Borough during an acrimonious FA Cup Fourth Round saga in 1988. The first referred to a disputed Alan Shearer goal and the second to the choice of match ball, a pre-game talking point.

One ball in Barnsley,
There's only one ball in Barnsley.

> Spurs fans, to the tune of 'Guantanamera', ridicule a lengthy
> hold-up in play while the ball is retrieved from the back of a
> stand during an FA Cup replay in February 1988.

One Hughes in London,
There's only one Hughes in London.

> Arsenal fans acclaim their two-goal hero Stephen Hughes
> in a Highbury win over Chelsea, who had Mark Hughes in
> their line-up, in 1998.

Cheer up Peter Reid,
Oh what can it mean,
To a Sunderland supporter,
To be top of the league.

> 'Daydream Believer', a hit for The Monkees in 1967, as revived by
> the Roker Roar in 1996.

Fuck off Peter Reid,
Oh what can it mean,
To the sad Mackem bastards,
And their shit football team.

> A Newcastle United version of the same song.

**They're walking home, they're walking home.
They're walking, Chelsea are walking home.**

> One of the many 'Three Lions' variations that surfaced in the 1996-
> 97 season, this chant was directed at the Stamford Bridge faithful by
> fans of Newcastle United after the stadium Tannoy announced a
> forthcoming tube strike.

**When Wise went up to lift the FA Cup,
We were there, we were there.
When Wise went up to lift the FA Cup,
We were there, we were there.**

> Chelsea fans celebrate their 1997 FA Cup win over Middlesbrough.

We'll never go to Dublin.

Are you listening Joe Kinnear?

> Wimbledon fans air their trenchant views on a proposed
> move to the Irish Republic in 1997.

**Vialli, whoah-oh, Vialli, whoah-oh,
He came from Italy, to play for Chelsea.**

**Vierra, whoah-oh, Vierra, whoah-oh,
He came from Senegal, to play for the Arsenal.**

> Bobby Rydell's 1960 hit 'Volare' enjoyed an unlikely renaissance at two London
> football grounds in the late Nineties, Chelsea and Arsenal fans respectively
> singing the praises of their overseas imports Gianluca Vialli and Patrick Vierra.

You're not fit,
You're not fit,
You're not fit to wear the shirt,
You're not fit to wear the shirt.

> Sung, to the tune of 'Bread Of Heaven', by disgruntled Aston Villa fans at
> Ewood Park as their team were humbled 5-0 by Blackburn Rovers.

Easy, easy, easy, easy!

> Chanted by the same fans seven days later as Villa crushed local
> rivals West Bromwich Albion 4-0 in the FA Cup.

Dance, dance, wherever you may be,
We signed a young kid from Torquay,
He soon settled and he soon made his mark,
He's the boy we call Lee Sharpe,
He danced at the Villa where two goals he did score,
He danced in the derby where we only got a draw,
He danced round the Scousers and the Leeds
    'cause they're shite,
And round the the boys in red and white.

> While Lee Sharpe celebrated his goals with an Elvis routine involving a cor-
> ner flag, Old Trafford celebrated his wing play with this version of 'Lord Of
> The Dance'. The 'boys in red and white' are Arsenal, against whom Sharpe
> once netted a League Cup hat-trick at Highbury.

You are my Solskjaer, my only Solskjaer,
You make me happy when skies are grey,
Alan Shearer was fucking dearer,
But please don't take my Solskjaer away.

> The United hordes sing the praises of their young Norwegian striker
> to the strains of 'You are My Sunshine'.

I'm thinking of the Dave,
A Cockney lad, who isn't bad, believe me.

They're red, immense, our future, our defence,
Phil and Gaz, Phil and Gaz.

When the Reds score a goal and it's not Andy Cole,
It's Poborsky.
When the ball hits the net, though his hair's not
   cut yet,
It's Poborsky.

We'll drink, we'll drink, we'll drink,
To Eric The King, The King, The King,
'Cause he's the leader of our football team,
He's the greatest French footballer,
That the world has ever seen.

If you go down to the White Hart Lane,
You'd better go in disguise
If you go down to the White Hart Lane,
You'll never believe your eyes,
'Cause Uncle Ted is wearing red,
And Gerry wishes he was dead,
'Cause today's the day,
That Sheringham scores a hat-trick.

Five of the finest chants penned by Manchester United super-fan
Pete Boyle (see Chapter Four). The first honours David Beckham,
the second the Neville brothers, the third – to the tune of Dean
Martin's 'That's Amore' – is dedicated to Karel Poborsky, the
fourth marks the coronation of Cantona while the fifth commem-
orates Teddy Sheringham's move from White Hart Lane to Old
Trafford. The England striker actually missed a penalty on his
United debut – ironically at White Hart Lane – resulting in an
updated version of the last two lines which ran 'today's the day
that Sheringham misses a spot-kick'.

Bring back the Fifties!

> Wolves fans recall their side's glory years during a demonstration
> against manager Graham Taylor.

We're so broke it's unbelievable.

> Tottenham fans at the 1991 FA Cup Final.

Are you watching, Hartlepool?

> Darlington fans celebrate winning the GM Vauxhall Conference, and a
> return to the Football League, in May 1990.

Don't you think we've had enough?

> Birmingham fans, to the tune of 'Bread Of Heaven', during a 3-0
> defeat by Cambridge.

Oleg, Oleg, give us a wave.

> Rangers fans welcome Oleg Kuznetsov, an uncomprehending
> Ukrainian signing, in 1990.

We'll win again, don't know where, don't know when.

> Sheffield United fans recall Vera Lynn during a poor run in 1990.

We all agree, Fettis is better than Shearer.

> Hull fans sing their praises of their goalkeeper, and stand-in striker,
> Alan Fettis, who scored twice for the first team in 1995.

**Philippe, Philippe Albert,
Everyone knows his name.**

> Newcastle United fans remember the theme from 'Rupert The Bear'
> in singing to their Belgian defender Philippe Albert.

**Georgie Graham's magic,
He wears a magic hat.
And when he saw the FA Cup,
He said I'm having that.**

> Arsenal fans celebrate their 1993 FA Cup win to tune of 'My Old
> Man's A Dustman'.

Ian Wright, Wright, Wright!

> So good they named him three times. Highbury salutes Arsenal's
> record goalscorer to the rhythm of the the early Eighties soca hit
> 'Hot, Hot, Hot' by Arrow.

D. I. Canio!

> Both Celtic and Sheffield Wednesday fans harked back to Ottowan's
> dance hit 'D. I. S. C. O.' in acknowledging the imported skills of
> Italian striker Paolo Di Canio.

You've got mad cow disease.

> Taunted by repeated versions of the theme from 'The Dambusters',
> German fans at Euro 96 give their answer to the English ranks,
> complete with moo-ing noises.

'Blue Moon',
You started singing too soon,
You thought you'd beat us three-one,
And now Howard Kendall has gone.

Manchester United fans taunt their Maine Road rivals after the departure of City manager Howard Kendall in 1993. The Old Trafford side had also recovered from 1-3 down to draw 3-3 in one of the year's Manchester derbies.

And all the runs that Kinky makes are winding,
And all the goals that Uwe scores are blinding,
'Cause maybe, you're gonna be the one that saves me,
And after all, you're my Alan Ball.

Manchester City fans look to local heroes Oasis, and their epic single 'Wonderwall', in singing the praises of their side in 1995. The two players referred to are Georgiou Kinkladze and Uwe Rosler.

He's going to France, he's going to France,
He's going, Merson's going to France.

A 'Three Lions' variation, pushing the England claims of Middlesborough striker Paul Merson at the Tees-Wear derby against Sunderland in 1998. The in-form Merson was included in the next England squad.

You'll never play for England!

West Ham fans taunt Blackburn Rovers and England striker Chris Sutton during an FA Cup Fifth Round reply in 1998. Sutton had withdrawn from an England 'B' pool in protest at not being selected for the full squad.

Sutton for England!

The Ewood faithful restate Sutton's case for international recognition as the striker scores a hat-trick against Leicester City three days later.

IT'S ALL GONE QUIET OVER THERE

OVER THERE

The future of the football chant

P rior to the carnival of song that underscored the England and Scotland matches in *Euro 96*, it appeared that the golden era of the football chant was a thing of the past. The changes that have affected the game in the Nineties – in particular the predominance of expensive reserved seats, executive boxes, family sections, overzealous stewards and the growing restrictions on away fans – looked to have put an end to singing on the scale of the Sixties and Seventies. And, despite the atmosphere that reigned during *Euro 96*, many close observers of the game still believe that the heyday of football chanting is now over.

There remains a romance attached to the days when entire sections of a football crowd would sing in unison throughout a match: the sensation of thousands of people all willing the same thing to happen through their singing was a powerful one and it may be that football will never witness such an era again. Former club and international manager Tommy Docherty, who experienced the songs of both Stamford Bridge and Old Trafford from the dugout in the Sixties and Seventies, certainly believes the chants have dried up dramatically. 'There was a time when you would enjoy a football match just for the crowd,' said The Doc early in 1996. 'You might have been watching the most boring game of all time, but you would get a charge just from listening to the supporters chant and sing. But they don't sing anymore. These days, the atmosphere is so dead that they might as well be playing down the bloody mortuary.' Many fans and fanzine writers agree with The Doc's pessimistic assessment. 'There is a Mexican Wave effect with chanting these days' says Chelsea supporter Graeme. 'The songs take much longer to catch on. If a song starts at one end of the stadium, it takes so long to reach the other parts that the people who started have stopped.'

'The chants now are pretty mundane,' says Dave Woodhall of the Aston Villa fanzine *Heroes & Villains*. 'Maybe that is a reflection of some of the football that Villa have played in recent seasons. But there has also been a massive sea change in the club's supporters. On one hand, there are the old stalwarts who have been going to Villa Park for decades. Since *Italia 90*, however, there have also been a lot of people coming to Villa Park just to *watch* the atmosphere rather than help to create it.' For Mark Jensen, editor of Newcastle United fanzine *The Mag*, the constraints on travelling fans rather than the advent of all-seater stadia have been the biggest factor in changing the nature of singing at football.

'There are now more restrictions to ticket sales,' he says. 'Because of this, we're not getting the huge banks of away fans that the big clubs used to bring in the past. You don't get the same level of vocal competition between the fans. It used to run right through the match. Now, apart from the odd really big game, you only get that sheer volume occasionally. Only ten years ago, however, there would be a constant chorus of threats and tributes running for the whole match.'

The tragic football disasters of the Eighties – at Heysel, Bradford and Hillsborough – should always offset any excess of nostalgic sentiment advocating a return to terracing at big grounds. The imposing all-seater stadia that followed the Taylor report were an inevitable necessity. In terms of crowd safety, they have pulled Britain's football grounds out of the Victorian era and into the Nineties. There are some who believe the presence of seating in every stand will eventually accelerate the decline of the football chant. But the evidence of *Euro 96* and some of the singing since that particular tournament would suggest otherwise. There are also plenty of football watchers who believe that seats in themselves should not automatically thwart the singers.

'You can give the people seats, but you cannot force them to sit down,' said former Newcastle United manager Kevin Keegan. 'The fans want to sing. And, unless you are Val Doonican, you cannot do that sitting down.' Certain clubs, Arsenal among them, have attempted to introduce specific 'singing sections' for supporters. There have even been calls in some matchday programmes for 'songleaders' to come forward to help get the chants going. But, while undoubtedly well-intentioned, such plans are sadly doomed to failure in that they do not take account of the essentially spontaneous nature of the best football songs.

A much better idea would be an increase in the availability of unreserved seats, particularly behind the goals, which would allow the keenest fans to get to the ground early to commandeer the prime spots. Unreserved seating – which could still be sold beforehand and even made available on the same basis as season tickets – would also enable significant pockets of supporters to gather together inside grounds on an informal, impromptu basis. One of the integral aspects of the Sixties, Seventies and Eighties could be recreated without compromising crowd safety.

There are still odd, fleeting moments when the crowd at a big match can recreate the full vocal and visual splendour of the halcyon days of song. The Kop may never burst into the hits of The Beatles as they once did. But the communal raising of scarves just before kick-off on a Saturday afternoon at Anfield still offers a brief, tantalising, glimpse of how it must have been in the early Sixties. And, periodically, in a big match – whether it be at St James's Park, Old Trafford, Parkhead, Ibrox, Highbury, White Hart Lane or Wembley – the intensity and spontaneity of the great singing years is resurrected. In the big weekend Cup matches or vital midweek European ties, the atmosphere, songs and chants make their return.

'A football match without singing,' said one fan, 'is what the cinema must have been like before they discovered talkies. It must never happen.'

BIBLIOGRAPHY

BOOKS

The Story Of Football by Martin Tyler (Marshall Cavendish, 1978)
The Sunday Times Illustrated History Of Football by Chris Nawrat and Steve Hutchings (Reed International Books, 1995)
The Glory Game by Hunter Davies (Mainstream Publishing, 1985)
The Umbro Book Of Football Quotations by Peter Ball and Phil Shaw (Ebury Press, 1996)
Football Fan's Guide by Janet Williams and Mark Johnson (Collins Willow, 1995)
The Football Man by Arthur Hopcraft (Sports Pages, 1988)

MAGAZINES AND NEWSPAPERS

New Musical Express, Vox, Goal, Loaded and *The Glasgow Observer*

SELECTED DISCOGRAPHY

'Blue Monday' by Englandneworder (Factory/MCA single, 1990)
'Three Lions' by Baddiel & Skinner & Lightning Seeds (Epic single, 1996)
'Blue Day' by Suggs & Co. feat. the Chelsea Team (WEA single, 1997)
'Sharp As A Needle' by The Barmy Army (On-U Sound single, 1980)
'Touched By The Hand Of Cicciolina' by Pop Will Eat Itself (RCA single, 1990)
It's Like Everything Else by I Ludicrous (Kaleidoscope EP, 1987)
Flair *1989* (Confection album, 1989)
Bend It! 91, Bend It! 92, Bend It! 93 and *Bend It! 94* (Exotica albums)
Four-Two-Four (él album, 1989)
The Red Album – A Mancunian Fantasy (Exotica album, 1993)
Cantona – The Album (Exotica album, 1995)
Georgie – The Best Album (Exotica album, 1997)
Toon Army Tunes – Tribute to Newcastle Utd. (Cherry Red album, 1995)
Glory Glory Tottenham Hotspur (Cherry Red album, 1995)
Good Old Arsenal (Cherry Red album, 1996)
England's Glory (Cherry Red album, 1996)
You'll Never Walk Alone – 24 Anfield Anthems (Cherry Red album, 1996)
The Famous Glasgow Rangers (Cherry Red album, 1996)
Hail! Hail! Celtic (Cherry Red album, 1996)
The Kop Choir (Cherry Red album, 1997)
Blue Flag – A Tribute to Chelsea (Cherry Red album, 1997)
Keep Right On – Birmingham City (Cherry Red album, 1997)

VIDEO

The Official History Of Liverpool FC (BBC Enterprises, 1987)

ACKNOWLEDGEMENTS

Special thanks to all those who have helped directly with this book, including Phil Shaw, Pat Nevin, Kasy Keller, George Graham, Suggs, Ian Broudie, Peter Hooton, Pete Boyle, Graham Pell, Scott Getley and Tim Madgwick at Cherry Red, Jim Phelan at Exotica and Steve Beauchampe at the Football Supporters Association.

Additional thanks to James Brown, Paul Hawksbee, Sophie Sparrow, Paula Cocozza, Steve Kemsley, Jim White, Trevor Haylett, Julie Bland, Tim Ross, Barbara Charone, Martin Ling, David Stubbs, Angie Somerside, Chris Waddle, Kevin Cummins, John Colquhoun, David Belcher, Mark Jensen and Dave Woodhall.

Thanks to Jon Wilde for the inception and help with the prologue. Thanks to Jake Lingwood, Sarah Leisching and Jenny Dempsey at Ebury. Special thanks to Debra for her patience and support. And extra special thanks to Barny and Nancy for making it all worthwhile.

A NOTE FROM THE PUBLISHER

We would love to hear your comments on *You're Not Singing Anymore*, with a view to publishing a second volume of the book. If you have any interesting chant-related stories, or if your favourite chant is not included within these pages, do drop us a line at:

You're Not Singing Anymore
Ebury Press
Random House
20 Vauxhall Bridge Road
London SW1V 2SA.